Paul Gerhardt's Spiritual Songs Translated by John Kelly • Gerhardt, Paul

Publisher's Note

Purchase of this book entitles you to a free trial membership in the publisher's book club at www.rarebooksclub.com. (Time limited offer.) Simply enter the barcode number from the back cover onto the membership form on our home page. The book club entitles you to select from millions of books at no additional charge. You can also download a digital copy of this and related books to read on the go. Simply enter the title or subject onto the search form to find them.

Note: This is an historic book. Pages numbers, where present in the text, refer to the first edition of the book and may also be in indexes.

If you have any questions, could you please be so kind as to consult our Frequently Asked Questions page at www.rarebooksclub.com/faqs.cfm? You are also welcome to contact us there.
Publisher: General Books LLC™, Memphis, TN, USA, 2012. ISBN: 9781153825863.
Proofreading: pgdp.net

❦ ❦ ❦ ❦ ❦ ❦ ❦ ❦

CONTENTS.
PAGE
Preface 1
vii
Biographical Sketch 2
xi
Index of First Lines 8
xliii
Of the Holy Trinity 9
1
Advent 9
5
Birth of Christ—Christmas 11
14
Circumcision of Christ—New Year . 14
43
The Sufferings of Christ—Good Friday 15
49
Resurrection of Christ—Easter 18
71
Whitsuntide 19
78
Repentance 19
83
Prayer and the Christian Life 21
97
Songs of the Cross and Consolation 27
143
Songs of Praise and Thanksgiving ... 40
238
Morning and Evening Songs 44
270
Miscellaneous 46
289
Of Death, the Last Day, and Eternal Life 49
312
[vii]

PREFACE.

This volume contains a large selection from Paul Gerhardt's "Spiritual Songs." Every piece included is given in full, and is rendered into the metre of the original. A few of the following translations have appeared at various times during the last three years in different periodicals. They have been revised for this volume. Several of the hymns have been beautifully translated by others; and had the Translator been compiling a volume composed of selections from various authors, this might have formed a strong reason for not doing them again, but to have omitted them from a volume like the present would have been to give a selection from Gerhardt without some of his most celebrated productions; besides, in the other collections where they appear they are not all given in full, nor are they always rendered into the metre of the original, [vi-ii] save in those published with the music attached. As far as the Translator is aware, the greater number of the following songs have never appeared in an English dress before.

Every one who has reflected on the subject, or attempted metrical translation, knows that literality is rarely attainable, that a certain measure of freedom must be used. The Translator has, however, striven to maintain fidelity to the sense of the original, and has occasionally somewhat sacrificed euphony to fidelity.

It is not to be expected that the people's poet of one nation and of a former age will become, through translation, the people's poet of another nation in a later generation. Individual translations may win for themselves a place side by side with the favourite songs of native growth. Instances of this will occur to every one familiar with our hymnology; but this can hardly happen in many cases. The translations on the principle of this volume may neither be uninteresting nor unedifying on that account, and it may be permitted to the Translator to trust that Paul Gerhardt in his present dress may be found stimulating and refreshing [ix] to many. Gerhardt was peculiarly a son of consolation. The Translator has found him so in the hour of trial, and he will feel repaid if he should become the cup-bearer of the rich wine of consolation contained in the hymns of the staunch old German Lutheran to any English Christian readers "who may be in any wise afflicted."

The work of translation has been a labour of love. It has been the recreation of leisure hours from graver duties, and occasionally the occupation of days of unwilling, but unavoidable, total or partial freedom from professional engagements.

The edition used in this translation was Wackernagel's "Paulus Gerhardt's Geistliche Lieder getreu nach der bei seinen Lebzeiten erschienenen Ausgabe wiederabgedrückt. Neue Auflage, in Taschenformat."—Stuttgart, Verlag von Samuel Gottlieb Liesching, 1855. This edition has been followed in the classification and titles both of the sections and hymns.

The principal sources whence the materials for the biographical sketch have been drawn are "Paul Gerhardt's Geistliche Andachten, &c., mit Anmerkungen, [x] einer Geschichtlichen Einleitung und Urkunden herausgegaben, von Otto Schultze."—Berlin, 1842. "Paul Gerhardt, nach seinem Leben und Wirken, aus zum Theile ungedrückten Nachrichten dargestellt," von E. G. Roth, Pastor Primarius zu Luebben in der Niederlausitz.—Leipzig, 1829.

Feustking, Langbecker, Herzog, and others were also read, or more or less consulted.
[xi]

BIOGRAPHICAL SKETCH.

Paul Gerhardt was born in Graefenhainichen in Electoral Saxony, where his father, Christian Gerhardt, was Burgomaster. There is some doubt as to the precise year of his birth, owing to the destruction of the church books when the place was burnt by the Swedes on the 16th of April, 1637. According to some, the event took place in the year 1606; according to others, in 1607. The probability is in favour of the former date, for General Superintendent Goltlob Stolze, of Lübben, says that he died, in the 70th year of his age, in the year 1676.

There is no information concerning his youth and education. He was still very young when the Thirty Years' War broke out, and his preparation for his profession and entrance on it took place in those troublous times, which may account for his late settlement in a ministerial sphere. In the year 1651, when in his forty-fifth year, we find him still only a [xii] candidate of theology, and resident as a tutor in the family of Andreas Bertholdt, Chancery Advocate in Berlin, whose daughter he subsequently married. In that year a vacancy occurred in the ministry at Mittenwald, by the death of Probst Caspar Göde. The magistracy of that place applied to the clergy of Berlin to recommend a suitable man to them for the office. Paul Gerhardt was their unanimous choice. They recommended him as an honourable, estimable, and learned man, whose diligence and erudition were known, of good parts and incorrupt doctrine, of a peace-loving disposition and blameless Christian life, which qualities had procured for him the love of all classes, high and low, in Berlin. They furthermore added that he had frequently, at their friendly invitation, exercised the excellent gifts with which God had endowed him for the edification of the church, and had thereby deserved well of the people, and endeared himself to them. The clergy met together for consultation, and sent this recommendation to Mittenwald without the knowledge of Gerhardt; no higher testimony, therefore, could have been given to his character, learning, and abilities. [xiii] He was accordingly appointed and set apart to his office in St. Nicholas' Church, Berlin, on the 18th of November, 1651, and entered before the close of the year on his duties. The church book which he kept from Jan. 1, 1652, till Dec. 31, 1656, bears testimony to his fidelity and conscientiousness in the discharge of this part of the duties of his office.

On February 11th, 1655, he was married to Anna Maria, daughter of the Chancery Advocate Bertholdt, in whose family he had been tutor. Before he left Mittenwald, his first child, a daughter, was born and died. There is a slab to her memory still standing in the church. Several circumstances in his position at Mittenwald conspired to make Gerhardt desire a change, and welcome a translation to Berlin when an opportunity offered. The relation between his colleague, Deacon Allborn, and himself was not friendly: Allborn had been passed over by the magistrates in favour of Gerhardt. The want of cordiality which prevailed in consequence must have been very trying to a man of Gerhardt's disposition. The income of the office was also small, and his circumstances consequently straitened. His ties and associations in Berlin would also be strong inducements of themselves to the acceptance of an appointment there.
[xiv]

The welcome relief came when the magistrates appointed him to the third Diaconate of St. Nicholas' Church, vacant by the death of Probst Peter Vher, and the consequent promotion of the other ministers. The spirit in which he received and accepted the invitation is shown in his letter to the magistrates on accepting their offer. He humbly and gratefully recognized the hand of God in the matter; and, owning his own weakness, earnestly solicited the prayers of the faithful. His letter is dated June 4, 1657, and in the register of St. Nicholas there is an entry of a baptism made by him on the 22nd of July. Consequently he must have entered on his duties soon after. Gerhardt, doubtless, joyfully returned to Berlin, anticipating a happy ministry there; but it was there his greatest trials awaited him. These trials arose out of the measures taken by Frederick William, at that time Elector of Brandenburg, to allay the animosity prevailing between the adherents of the Lutheran and Reformed Confessions respectively. The feud was of long standing, and the efforts made to heal it had been hitherto in vain.

With the laudable desire of pacifying party strife, [xv] the Elector appointed a conference to be held between the Lutheran and Reformed clergy of Berlin and Cöln-on-the-Spree, under the direction of the Lord President, Baron Otto von Schwerin, on the Reformed side, and Chancellor Lorenz Christian von Somnitz, of Pomerania, and others, on the Lutheran side. The Lutheran clergy of the three chief churches in Berlin and Cöln, and the Reformed court preachers, Bartholomew Stosch and Johann Kunschius, the rector of the Joachimsthal Gymnasium, and the philologue Joh. Vorstius, constituted the membership of the conference. Kunschius, being soon after summoned to accompany the Elector to Königsberg, took no part in the conferences, and his place was filled by Gerson Vechner, of the Joachimsthal Gymnasium.

The object of the Conference, according to the Electoral Rescript, was to consider the following points:—

I. Whether in the Reformed Confessions, particularly in those named in the last Electoral Edict (January 2nd, 1662), viz.:—The Confessio Sigismundi, the Colloquium Lipsiacum, the Declaratio Thoruniensis,—anything is taught or affirmed, in teaching, believing, or affirming which any one is, *judicio divino*, accursed.

II. Whether anything is denied or passed over in [xvi] silence, without acknowledging or practising which no one could be saved.

The Berlin clergy were reluctant to enter on the conference. They thought that as it concerned the Church of the Mark generally it should not be limited to Berlin and Cöln, and that it was a subject requiring mature consideration. At length, however, having protested in vain, they consented, but manifestly determined to concede nothing.

The conference met at various times during the years 1662-63. Gerhardt took no public part. The speaking devolved first on Probst Lilius, but soon afterwards, and for the remainder of the meetings, on Archdeacon Reinhardt. Gerhardt wrote a judgment unfavourable to the conferences, because he thought nothing but syncretism would come out of it—*i.e.*, the confusion of the two confessions, into which the Rinteln theologians had permitted themselves to be seduced. By his votes he evinced his interest in all its proceedings.

As might be surmised, from the state of party feeling, the conference was not only fruitless, but left [xvii] matters in a worse condition than they were when it first met. Furthermore, at the last sitting but one, on the 22nd of May, 1663, the Berlin clergy incurred the high displeasure of the Elector, by defending and approving the conduct of their speaker Reinhardt on an occasion when he had given great offence to his Highness. It is thought, that at this time Gerhardt wrote his heart-stirring and beautiful hymn,— Ist Gott für mich, so trete? (
Is God for me, t'oppose me? 36
) The Elector, in consequence of the result of the conferences, issued an edict on the 16th of September, 1664, in substance the same but more stringent than the previous one. All were required to pledge themselves to obedience to this edict, whereas subscription to the former one had been required only from candidates at ordination. The edict required the clergy of both confessions, on pain of dismissal from office and other penalties, to refrain from vituperating each other, from deducing absurd and impious doctrines from each other's dogmas, and imputing them to their opponents. The edict also commanded that the ordinance of baptism should be administered without exorcism, when the parents desired it. The edict produced the most profound consternation. It was regarded as endangering religious liberty and the freedom of conscience. The [xviii] Lutheran preachers felt themselves hampered by it in the discharge of their duties. Regarding, as they did, their symbolical books and ecclesiastical customs as sacred things, using their authorized formularies in the instruction of the people, and introducing the element of controversy largely into their ministrations, they felt themselves quite crippled in the discharge of their functions. It seemed to them that if they gave up their liberty in the pulpit, they would be necessitated to give up their customs also, and so violate their solemn obligations. They thought that compliance would imperil the Lutheran Church, the welfare of their congregations, and the peace of their own souls. Such was the view taken of the matter by many strict and conscientious men. We cannot help thinking that their view was mistaken and exaggerated, that these things were not endangered, that it was perfectly possible for them to have been loyal to their church, to have instructed their people faithfully in all the peculiar doctrines of their system, and yet have rendered obedience to the Electoral edict. Many were actually conducting themselves both according to its letter and spirit, and yet were filled with those alarms which we must call groundless, at the very thought of binding themselves by a pledge to [xix] act as they were doing. While we hold them to have been mistaken, we cannot but respect their fidelity to their honest convictions, and their fortitude in accepting the sad consequences,—the severing of the ties that bound them to beloved flocks, the loss of office and emolument, and expatriation. The principles of toleration were not rightly understood, either by the Church or State at the time.

As we read the painful annals of the time, the thought often arises in the mind, how much better had it been if the evil which it was the laudable intention of the Elector to correct, had been permitted to work its own cure. There were doubtless many, who had given too much cause for complaint by the licence they allowed themselves in the pulpit in attacking their theological adversaries, but those who suffered most would probably be those, who, like Gerhardt, were not open to reproach, yet felt themselves constrained by conscience to refuse obedience to the Elector's command. Hundreds signed the edict. Some who had scruples yielded on account of their wives and children. There was a witticism current at the time which was put into the mouths of the pastors' wives:—

"Schreibt, Schreibt,

Lieber Herre, auf dass ihr bei der Pfarre bleibt."
[xx]
Which may be freely and roughly rendered,—

"Subscribe, subscribe, dear husband, do!

Lest you must from the parish go."
Very many, however, were thrown into the greatest distress of mind, and could not obey and preserve a good conscience. The Berlin ministers sought the opinion of various theological faculties and churches on the crisis.

The Elector, ignorant of the trouble given to the consciences of many worthy men, viewed this conduct on their part as self-willed, and an unwarrantable opposition to what appeared to him a needful regulation. He ordered Lilius and Reinhardt to be removed from office, if they delayed to subscribe, and gave the others time for consideration. The two former, failing to obey, were deposed.

Gerhardt, with the three others who

were threatened, turned to the magistracy, and solicited their good offices in intercession with the Elector. The magistrates represented to the Elector that the Berlin clergy had observed the edict, but that they objected to subscription; they begged the Elector not to enforce subscription on those already in office, as it would tend to compromise them with the people and foreign churches; they furthermore stated, that obedience rests not so much in [xxi] subscription and in the letter, as in the mind and in deed. They begged him to reinstate Lilius and Reinhardt in office.

The Berlin clergy presented a petition, substantially to the same effect, at the same time. They stated, in addition, that the Reformed clergy had not been compelled to sign. The only result of this petition was, that the Reformed were forthwith commanded to subscribe the edict.

The ministers, in another document, set forth their scruples at large, but thereby only incurred the further displeasure of the Elector. The deposition of Lilius and Reinhardt, however, caused such an uproar, that the Elector issued a declaration on May 4, 1665, setting forth the seasons of his procedure. Further efforts were made, and the result was, that time was allowed to Lilius to reconsider his refusal, and in the beginning of the following year he subscribed. On account of his compliance, he became the object of the most bitter and galling attacks, and did not long survive. The last days of the old man were embittered by the treatment he received at the hands of zealous, but uncharitable Lutherans, and death was doubtless a welcome event to him. In the case of Reinhardt, the result was only a more severe sentence. He was banished [xxii] from the town, forbidden to maintain any correspondence with it, and the magistrates were ordered to fill up the vacancy caused by his removal. He removed to Leipzig, where he was chosen to the pastorate of St. Nicholas' Church, and was subsequently made Professor of Theology, which office he held till his death, in 1669.

Paul Gerhardt was the next minister who was called on to subscribe the edict. The Elector was convinced that, next to Reinhardt, he was the most vehement opponent of peace between the Lutheran and Reformed. When Reinhardt was reproached in the Consistory with inciting his colleagues to resistance, Gerhardt said, with some warmth, that it was not so, that he had encouraged Reinhardt when he showed a disposition to yield; he was older in years, and had been longer in office, and he should be sorry to follow others. It was also said, that during an illness which befell him, he sent for his colleagues, and earnestly warned them not to subscribe the bond pledging them to observance of the edict. These things were, at least, carried to the Elector, and prejudiced him against Gerhardt. On the same day that Lilius was reinstated in office, Gerhardt was cited to appear before the Consistory (Feb. 6th, 1666), and called upon to sign. Eight days were allowed [xxiii] him for consideration, and in the first instance he accepted the delay, but before the rising of the same session, he declared that he had had ample time for consideration, and that he could not change his mind, whereupon he was deposed from office, in the name of the Elector.

Great as was the agitation produced in the public mind by the deposition of Lilius and Reinhardt, the sensation occasioned by Gerhardt's was much more profound. He was the most beloved, as well as most celebrated, of all the ministers. Measures were immediately taken by the community in his favour. The citizens and the guilds of the cloth-makers, bakers, butchers, tailors, and pewterers, united to petition the magistrates in favour of exemption for Gerhardt. They said that every one knew that he had never spoken against the faith and the co-religionists of the Elector, much less vituperated them, but that he had sought to lead every one to true Christianity, and had never attacked any one in word or deed.

The magistrates, on presenting this representation to the Elector, on the 13th of February, added:—"He has not thought of the Reformed, much less insulted them; he has maintained a blameless walk, giving offence to no one, so much so, that his Highness, without [xxiv] any suspicion, had admitted his songs into the hymn-book for the Mark, in 1658. Should a man so pious, so intellectual, so celebrated in many lands, leave the town, it was to be feared that grave thoughts would be excited in the minds of foreigners, and that God would visit them for it. If he refused subscription, it would not be imputed to disobedience, but to scruples of conscience, seeing that before the publication of the edict he had fulfilled its object by his modest behaviour." The Prince, in reply, stated that he had sufficient grounds for enforcing the provisions of the edict, and that Gerhardt must comply with them, or bear the penalty.

A second petition was got up in his favour, in which, in addition to the above guilds, the carpenters, cutlers, armourers, and coppersmiths joined. As this petition also was unfavourably received, the States of the Mark took up the cause of the deposed. "The dismissal of Gerhardt," they informed the Elector, on the 27th of July, 1666, "excited great fear in the country for religion, for this man is recognized by the adherents of both confessions as a pious, exemplary, and, without doubt, a peace-loving theologian, against whom no charge can be brought save his refusal to subscribe the edicts."
[xxv]
The Elector yielded at length. After his return from Cleve, he summoned the magistrates to appear before him, on January 9th, 1667, at three o'clock in the afternoon; and through the Lord President, Otto von Schwerin, in presence of several privy councillors, made the desired, but hardly expected announcement, that as there was no complaint against Paul Gerhardt, save that he refused to subscribe the edicts, his Electoral Highness must believe that he has misunderstood the purport of them; he, therefore, restored him to his office, and absolved him from the necessity of subscription.

Immediately after the audience, the Elector sent a private secretary to Gerhardt, to convey the intelligence to him, and to say at the same time that his Highness cherished the confident expectation that he would act conformably to the edicts, without subscription, and continue to manifest his known moderation. Next day the magistrates, delighted with the grace of the Prince, hastened to inform Gerhardt of his unconditional restoration to office, and on the 12th of January, the joyous event was announced in the *Sunday Mercury*, a weekly paper very much read in Berlin at that time. But the private message from the Elector threw Gerhardt into fresh distress of mind. He felt hampered by the condition still attached to his restoration to [xxvi] office, and he applied to the magistrates to aid him in discovering the exact terms of his restoration. In his letter to the magistrates, he expressed his earnest desire to spend the remainder of his life among his flock, if he could do so with a good conscience, saying how wretched a thing it was to hold office with an uneasy conscience. He knew the anxieties incident to the faithful discharge of the pastoral office, and said, that he would be the most wretched man on earth if to them were added the reproaches of a guilty conscience. His desire was not in the very least to appear to depart from his previous mode of teaching, and from the customs of his church, which, as a Lutheran clergyman, he had sworn to maintain. Referring to the moderation which had been so commended in him, he said, "I have never understood it, and never can understand it otherwise, than that I shall be permitted to remain faithful to my Lutheran confessions of faith, and especially to the 'Formula Concordiae,' and that I am not required to regard any of them, or permit others to regard any one of them, as a dishonourable, injurious, or blasphemous book."

The magistrates sent him a copy of the decree reinstating him in office, hoping thereby to remove his scruples. He made a further representation to the [xxvii] magistrates on the 26th of January, 1667. In this he pointed out how the decree ascribed his refusal to a misunderstanding of the edicts, and that, though absolved from subscription, he was bound by them still; that he could only understand the edicts literally; that he could not re-enter his office with any other conscience than he had first entered it with; he could not inflict on himself the wound on re-entrance into office which he had, in the strength of the Holy Ghost, patiently and silently endured a year's suspension to avoid; that if his conscience permitted him to yield obedience he would subscribe the edicts, "for," said he, "what I can do with a good conscience, I can easily consent and promise to do." He begged them to intercede for him with the Prince, that he might be absolved from obedience to the edicts on resuming office. In everything else he promised all possible hearty and humble obedience. He begged that he might be permitted to adhere to his Lutheran Confessions and "Formula Concordiae;" that he might so instruct his flock, and pledge himself to no other moderation than was rooted in these confessions. Only on these terms, he said, could he consent to preach. Gerhardt also wrote to the Elector to the same effect.

The magistrates resolved once more to apply to the [xxviii] Elector. They briefly stated the case, and begged his Highness to relieve Gerhardt's scruples. The Elector, on the very same day, returned their statement to the magistrates, with these words written on the margin:—"If the preacher, Paul Gerhardt, will not resume the office so graciously vouchsafed to him again, by his Serene Electoral Highness, for which he will have to answer to the Most High God, let the magistrates of Berlin, at their earliest convenience, invite some other able and peace-loving persons to preach as candidates; but let them not call any one until they have first humbly made known his qualifications to his Serene Highness.—Cöhl-on-the-Spree, Feb. 4th, 1667.—(Signed) Friederich Wilhelm ."

Gerhardt resigned his office, and so ended his ministry in Berlin. So great was the love his former flock bore to him that they still continued to contribute to his support.

It is commonly believed, that after his deposition in Berlin, he was invited to Saxe-Merseberg by Duke Christian, and that, on refusing the offer, the Duke granted him a pension. Otto Schultze, one of his biographers, and seemingly the most careful and thorough of them, says that he was unable to find any certain testimony to either of these facts. It seems [xxix] strange that he should refuse to go to Saxe-Merseberg, when, a short time after, he unhesitatingly accepted an invitation from the magistrates of Lübben, which was in the territories of Duke Christian; and in his correspondence with the magistrates of Lübben there is no reference to such an invitation from the Duke. The fact of his refusal, in the first instance, and his ready acceptance in the second, might be accounted for, however, by the death of his wife, which took place in March, 1668, whereby one very strong tie that bound him to Berlin was severed.

A story is told about this period of his life, and was for a long time received as an undoubted fact, which is so romantic that we could almost wish it were true. It is said, that having no certain dwelling-place, he set out with his wife and family to return to his fatherland, Electoral Saxony; that one evening his wife was sitting in the hotel where they were staying for the night, bemoaning her hard lot. Gerhardt in vain endeavoured to console her, and quoted Psalm xxxvii. 5, to her. Touched by the words himself, he went and sat down on a garden seat and wrote the song, "Commit whatever grieves thee ," &c., and came and read it to his wife, who was immediately [xxx] comforted. Later in the evening the Duke of Saxe-Merseberg's messengers arrived, bearing a letter to Gerhardt, offering him a pension, till he was otherwise provided for. They were glad when they found out who Gerhardt was, and handed him the letter, which he in turn handed to his wife, saying, "Did I not tell you to commit your ways unto the Lord?" Unfortunately for this story, the hymn in question had been published in 1666, and the story is otherwise inconsistent with the known facts of his history. The story is equally groundless, that this hymn was the means of procuring him an invitation from the Elector to return to Berlin.

The magistrates of Lübben, hearing of him, invited him to preach there, as a candidate for the vacant archdiaconate. He went thither and preached before them on October 14th, 1668. The next day he was informed as to the income, inspected the official residence, expressed his willingness to accept the appointment, and was assured that it would be offered to him. He then returned to Berlin. He did not take up his residence in Lübben until June in the following year, [xxxi] owing partly to domestic affliction, and partly to the vexatious delay in preparing his official house for his reception, arising from the dilatoriness and indifference of the magistrates in the matter. He had expressed hope, when he saw the house, which was unfit for any minister to live in, and not large enough for his family, that a more convenient one might be provided. He was assured that a deacon's house adjoining wonld be added to it. A friend visited Lübben some time after his appointment, and the work was not begun, nor even at a later period, when he himself went over. No sympathy was manifested towards him. He was asked if he wished to recede from his promise, and whether he wished a house *pro dignitate*; and was told that they did not know he had so large a household, and that what had been good enough before might be good enough still. All this must have been exceedingly annoying and humiliating to Gerhardt. Other points were raised with reference to the details of his ministerial duties; but leaving them for friendly settlement after his entrance on his office, he simply claimed that a house, not *pro dignitate*, but *pro necessitate*, should be prepared. A full statement of the case, addressed by him to the Government President, Alex. von Hoymb, at length produced the desired effect.
[xxxii]
He took the oath of religion before the Consistory on the 6th of June, and entered on the duties of his office on the third Sunday in Trinity. Gerhardt, in these transactions, appears to great advantage, in the reasonableness of his demands, and the manner he dealt with the ungenerous imputations made upon his motives and character. He would have removed to Lübben sooner had there been a suitable house to be got; but there was none. He laid stress, in his correspondence, on the want of a study in the Archdeacon's house, and insisted on the necessity of having a place for meditation and prayer, if he was to discharge his duties aright.

There are no written records concerning his work in Lübben. Dim tradition says, that he was often melancholy, that in these moods he would betake himself to the church, and kneeling before the crucifix, seek strength in fervent prayer. Feustking (who was almost his contemporary), General Superintendent in Anhalt-Zerbst, says, in the preface to his edition of his songs,—"Along with his piety Gerhardt had the devil, the false world, and the enemies of religion continually on his neck, with which he had to contend on the right and on the left, day and night. He also prayed very diligently, as earnestly as one pleads with his father. At the close of his life he had pious Arndt's 'Prayer [xxxiii] and Paradise Garden' continually before him, and so highly did he esteem it, that he wrote several hymns on its contents."

Many of Gerhardt's songs appeared in the first instance in various hymn-hooks. The first complete edition was published by J. E. Ebeling, Director of Music in the chief church in Berlin, in ten folio parts, each containing twelve songs, in 1666-67. It seems that Gerhardt never derived any pecuniary advantage from their publication. Tradition says, that after a warm conflict with the enemy he wrote the hymn "Wach auf mein Herz und Singe ," in proof of which the second verse is quoted. But he wrote no song after leaving Berlin. Schultze mentions that there is no song bearing his name that had not been printed in 1667.

His will, and the rules of life, written before his death, for his son Paul Friedrich, are worthy of quotation, revealing as they do the piety, simplicity, purity, integrity, and also the narrowness of his character. After expressing his gratitude to God for all the goodness and truth shown him from his mother's womb till that hour (he had then reached [xxxiv] his seventieth year), his hope of speedy deliverance from this life and entrance into a better, and praying God when his time came to take his soul into His Fatherly hands and grant his body quiet rest till the last day, when he should be reunited with those gone before as well as those left behind, and behold Jesus face to face, in whom he had believed though he had not seen Him, he goes on to say:—

"To my only son I leave few earthly possessions, but an honourable name, of which he will have no special reason to be ashamed.

"My son knows, that from tender infancy I gave him to the Lord my God as His own, that he should be a servant and preacher of His Holy Word. Let it be so, and let him not turn aside because he may have few good days therein, for God knows how to compensate for outward trial by inward gladness of heart and joy in the Holy Ghost. Study sacred theology in pure schools and incorrupt universities, and beware of Syncretists, for they seek the things of time, and are faithful neither to God nor man. In thine ordinary life, follow not bad company, but the will and commandment of thy God. In particular
[xxxv]
"1. Do nothing evil in the hope that it will remain secret,

'For nothing can so small be spun

That it comes not to the sun.'

"2. Never grow angry out of thine office and calling.

"If thou findest that anger hath inflamed thee, be perfectly silent, and do not utter a word until thou hast first repeated to thyself the Ten Commandments and the Christian Creed.

"3. Be ashamed of sinful, fleshly lusts; and when thou comest to years that thou canst marry, do so seeking direction from God, and the good counsel of pious, faithful, and judicious persons.

"4. Do people good whether they can

requite you or not, for what men cannot requite the Creator of Heaven and earth has long ago requited, in that He created thee, hath given thee His dear Son, and in holy baptism hath received and adopted thee as His son and heir.

"5. Flee covetousness like hell. Be content with what thou hast acquired with honour and a good conscience, though it may not be too much. Should God grant thee more, pray Him to preserve thee from any hurtful misuse of temporal possessions.

[xxxvi]

Summa; pray diligently, study something honourable, live peacefully, serve honestly, and remain steadfastly in thy faith and confession. So wilt thou one day die and leave this world willingly, gladly, blessedly! Amen."

He died on the 7th of June, 1676, as the Lübben church-book testifies, after he had been seven years in Lübben and twenty-five in the ministry.

It is said, that he died with the words of one of his own hymns on his lips. "Death can never kill us even," from verse 8th of the Christian Song of Joy. "Why should sorrow ever grieve me?" He is buried in the chief church, probably near the altar, though the precise spot cannot be determined. A portrait in oil, hung up in the church, testifies to the estimation in which he was held by the congregation, for besides his, there are only the portraits of a few General Superintendents, and none of any of his predecessors in office.

Towards the side, at the foot of the picture are the words:—

"Theologus in cribro Satanae versatus."

[xxxvii]

And under that again, the following epigram written by J. Wernsdorf:—

"Sculpta quidem Pauli, viva est atque imago Gerhardti,

Cujus in ore, fides, spes, amor usque fuit.

Hic docuit nostris Assaph redivivus in oris

Et cecinit laudes, Christe benigne, tuas.

Spiritus aethereis veniet tibi sedibus hospes,

Haec ubi saepe canes Carmina Sacra Deo."

It is not known what became of his son, and nothing is known of his posterity.

The editor of the Selection of Gerhardt's Songs—Bremen, 1817—states in his preface: "There is at present living in Bremen a great-granddaughter of Gerhardt's, eighty-one years of age, a simple Christian soul. Her father was, as she says, an advocate in Oldenburg; of her ancestor the poet she has neither written nor oral information."

There are three of Gerhardt's sermons extant in the library of the gymnasium of the Grey Cloister in [xxxviii] Berlin; and the titles and texts of three more are known. They are all funeral sermons. We would close this notice of the life of Gerhardt with a few extracts from Wackernagel's preface to his edition of Gerhardt's Spiritual Songs.

"Paul Gerhardt," he says, "may be viewed in a one-sided manner, from two quite opposite points of view, in relation to the spiritual contents of his songs. His poems appear to mirror the transition character of his age, when the personal life of the feelings, the subjective tendency, began to assert itself beside the Christian consciousness of the congregation. He may therefore be regarded as the last and the most perfect of those poets who were grounded in the ecclesiastico-confessional faith, and with him the line of the strict ecclesiastical poets closes. He may also be regarded as beginning the line of those in whose songs, praise and adoration of the revealed God recede before the expression of the feelings that master the soul in contemplating its relation to God revealing Himself to it as its salvation. The true view is, that Gerhardt stood in the fore front of his age and united in himself in the most lively manner both tendencies. Though he did not write so expressly for the congregation, so immediately in the interest of the church, [xxxix] as Luther, but from personal necessity, in personal temptations, yet the pulsation of his inner life was the common ecclesiastical confession; and his experiences, however personal they might be, were only waves of the flood of baptism and life which every other member of the church breathed and shared. His sorrow, and God's love, the soul's questions, and God's answers in him and in his songs, become one—so one as can only be when the experience is not only true for the individual, but also for the people and the church.

"For this reason Paul Gerhardt's are people's songs. They remind us sometimes of Friedrich Spee; above all, the glorious song,

'Go forth, my heart, and seek delight.'

But how much richer and more many-sided is the Evangelical than the Catholic poet, and at the same time better known and more familiar to the people! The Catholic congregations know nothing now of Friedrich Spee; but where is the Evangelical congregation that does not know Paul Gerhardt; in what churches are not his holy songs heard? What the pious Catherine Zell of Strasburg says of beautiful spiritual songs in her hymn-book is true of him:—'The [xl] journeyman mechanic at his work, the servant-maid washing her dishes, the ploughman and vinedresser in the fields, the mother by her weeping infant in the cradle, sing them.' High and low, poor and rich alike, find them equally consoling, equally edifying; in all stations, among young and old, there are examples to be found where some song of Gerhardt at particular periods in the history of the inner life was engraven for ever on the soul, and subsequently became the centre point of the dearest reminiscences. Winckleman's favourite song, even in Italy, after he had passed over to the Catholic Church, was,

'I sing to thee with heart and mouth.'

And once when he ordered a song-book from Germany, he was vexed, yea, exasperated, when he found that it did not contain this song.

"Schiller's mother nurtured the young mind of her son with the songs of our poet, with whom the song

'Now spread are evening shadows'

was a favourite,—the same song concerning which Johann Falk narrates that a beggar boy was preserved [xli] amid many temptations by singing to himself

the stanza commencing
'O Jesus! be my cover.'

"Books devoted to the exposition of spiritual songs, or to facts concerning pious persons, relate how many of Gerhardt's hymns have quickened many hearts in heavy affliction and anxiety, and have quietly composed their minds in the hour of death, and led them to peace.

"Above all, it was the mothers who fostered the domestic spiritual song, and handed down the old songs to the new generation. The noble picture of such a mother, even of his own, is sketched by T. F. Hippel, and the words in which she described the peculiarity of the poet to her son serve to portray herself as well as Gerhardt:—

"'After Luther, I must confess, I know no better hymn-poet than Gerhardt. He, Rist, and Dach form a trefoil, but the chosen instrument, Luther, was the root. Gerhardt wrote during the ringing of the church bells, so to speak. A certain impressiveness, a certain sorrowfulness, a certain fervour, were peculiar to him; he was a guest on earth, and everywhere in his one hundred and twenty-three songs sunflowers are sown. [xlii] This flower ever turns to the sun, so does Gerhardt to a blessed eternity.'

"The love with which the contemporaries of Gerhardt, as far as the bell of an evangelical church was heard, turned to his song, has only one precedent—the veneration, the devotion, with which Luther's songs were regarded. The songs of no other poet, either before or since, have ever produced so mighty an effect or obtained so speedy and so wide a circulation."
Wetzlar's "Analecta Hymnica."
One qualified and authorized to preach, but not ordained, ordination taking place only when the candidate is placed over a congregation as a pastor.
The Elector Sigismund had gone over to the Reformed Confession in 1613, and the position of the Lutherans and Reformed in the Mark in relation to the court had since been reversed.
Wackernagel says, that it was his official duty to sketch the writings in attack and defence, that they display great tact and acuteness, and furnish a new proof that critical acumen may be combined with a poetical temperament.
Since writing this sketch, the writer observes that currency has been given to this apocryphal story in a recent work, "Our Hymns: their Authors and their Origin. By the Rev. Josiah Miller."
In the reference to the Syncretists.
A Theologian experienced in the sieve of Satan.
A graven, indeed, yet living image of Paul Gerhardt,
   In whose mouth, faith, hope, love have ever been.
   Here Asaph returned to life, taught in our coasts, and sang thy praises, O Gracious Saviour!
   The Spirit will come to thee as a guest, from the heavenly seats wherever thou shalt sing these Sacred Songs to God.
[xliii]

INDEX OF FIRST LINES.
PAGE
A Lamb bears all its guilt away 49
A rest here have I never 316
After clouds we see the sun 261
Ah! faithful God, compass'nate heart 169
Ah! lovely innocence, how evil art thou deem'd 160
Awake, my heart! be singing 276
Be glad, my heart! now fear no more 329
Be joyful all, both far and near 75
Be thou contented! aye relying 202
Behold! behold! what wonder's here! 14
Bless'd is he the Lord who loveth 132
Bless'd is he who never taketh 130
By John was seen a wondrous sight 347
Come, and Christ the Lord be praising 24
Commit whatever grieves thee 225
Creator, Father, Prince of might! 109
Father of mercies! God most high 175
For Thee, Lord, pants my longing heart 88
Full of wonder, full of art 302
Full often as I meditate 143
Go forth, my heart, and seek delight 289
How can it be, my highest Light! 259
How heavy is the burden made 246
How long, Lord, in forgetfulness 235
I have deserv'd it, cease to oppose 165
I into God's own heart and mind 219
Immanuel! to Thee we sing 37
In grateful songs your voices raise 238
In prayer your voices raise ye 45
Is God for me? t'oppose me 208
Jesus! Thou, my dearest Brother 112
Let not such a thought e'er pain thee 83
Look up to thy God again 195
Lord God! Thou art for evermore 312
Lord, lend a gracious ear 92
Lord, Thou my heart dost search and try 138
Lord! to Thee alone I raise 135
Mine art Thou still, and mine shalt

be 333
My face, why shouldst thou troubled be 322
My God! my works and all I do 102
My heart! the seven words hear now 63
Now at the manger here I stand 32
Now gone is all the rain 298
Now spread are evening's shadows 285
Now with joy my heart is bounding 18
O Father! send Thy Spirit down 78
O God! from Thee doth wisdom flow 97
O God, my Father! thanks to Thee 117
O God! who dost Heaven's sceptre wield 294
O Jesus Christ! my fairest Light 122
O Lord! I sing with mouth and heart 255
O my soul, why dost thou grieve 155
Oh! bleeding head, and wounded 59
Oh, Jesus Christ! how bright and fair 307
On thy bier how calm thou'rt sleeping 338
Praise God! for forth hath sounded 251
Praise ye Jehovah 279
Say with what salutations 10
Scarce tongue can speak, ne'er human ken 1
See, world! thy Life assailèd 54
Shall I not my God be praising 240
The daylight disappeareth 282
The golden morning, joy her adorning 270
The Lord, the earth who ruleth 266
The time is very near 341
Thou art but man, to thee 'tis known 148
Thou must not altogether be 230
Thy manger is my paradise 26
'Tis patience must support you 184
Twofold, Father! is my pray'r 107
Up! up! my heart with gladness 71
What pleaseth God, my faithful child 189
Why should sorrow ever grieve me 214
Why should they such pain e'er give Thee 43
Why without, then, art Thou staying

5

SPIRITUAL SONGS

[1]

Of the Holy Trinity.

Scarce tongue can speak, ne'er human ken
    The myst'ry could discover,
That God, from His high throne to men
    Makes known the world all over:
    That He alone is King above
    All other gods whatever,
    Great, mighty, faithful, full of love,
    His saints doth aye deliver,
    One substance but three persons!
God, Father, Son, and Holy Ghost!
    The name thrice holy given,
    On earth by all the ransom'd host,
    And by the hosts of heaven.

[2]

He's Abraham's and Isaac's God,
    And Jacob's whom He knoweth,
    The Lord of Hosts, who every good
    Both night and day bestoweth,
    Who only doeth wonders!
His Son, from all eternity
    Begotten hath the Father,
    Who came as man, when God's decree
    Had fix'd, His sheep to gather.
    The Holy Ghost eternally,
    While all Their glory sharing,
    Their honour, pow'r, and majesty,
    A crown all equal wearing,
    Proceeds from Son and Father!
Be glad, my heart! thy portion see,
    Thy rich unequall'd treasure,
    He is thy Friend, supply will He
    Thy needs with bounteous measure.
    Who made thee in His image fair
    Thy load of guilt removeth,
    Gives thee His chosen's faith to share,
    Thy Joy in sorrow proveth,
    Through His own word most holy.

[3]

Bestir thyself, with all thy heart
    Thy God to know endeavour;
    Sweet rest such knowledge will impart,
    Thy soul with pure love ever
    Will cause to glow, and nourish thee
    For life and joy in heaven;
    Things heard of only here, shall be
    To open sight there given,
    By God to His dear children.
Woe! woe! to the besotted crew
    In wilful blindness living,
    Rejecting God, the honour due
    To Him, to creatures giving.
    The time will come when close shall He
    'Gainst them the door of heaven;
    Who God drive from them here, shall be
    By Him hereafter driven,
    From His high throne most holy!
O Prince of might! Thy mercy show,
    Thou God of earth and heaven,
    To every sinner here below
    May saving grace be given!

[4]

Bring back Thy sheep who go astray,
    And blinded eyes enlighten,
    And turn Thou every thing away
    That wickedly might frighten
    Thine own, whose faith is feeble.
Grant this, that we Thy people may
    All reach the heav'nly portals,
    And in Thy kingdom sing for aye,
    'Mid all the bless'd immortals:
    That Thou above art King alone
    All other gods high over,
    The Father, Son, and Spirit, One,
    Thy people's Shield and Cover,
    One substance but three persons!

[5]

Advent.

WHY WITHOUT, THEN, ART THOU STAYING?

Why without, then, art Thou staying,
    Blessed of the Lord from far?
    Enter now, no more delaying,
    Let it please Thee—Thou, my Star!
    Thou, my Jesus, Friend indeed,
    Helper in the hour of need!
    Saviour! ease the wounds that pain me,
    Let Thy comforts rich sustain me.
Lord, my wounds are pain and sorrow,
    That the hammer of the law
    With its terrors, night and morrow,
    Causeth, filling me with awe.
    Oh! the dreadful thunder peals
    When His anger God reveals,
    All my blood to tingle making,
    And my heart's foundation shaking!

[6]

Then with wiles the great deceiver
  Would to me all grace deny,
  Saying, in the hell for ever
  That torments him, I must be.
But I suffer sorer pangs,
  For with poison'd serpent fangs
  Doth my conscience gnawing, tearing,
  Stir remorse beyond all bearing.
Do I seek my woe to soften,
  And to lessen pain desire,
  With the world commingling often,
  Sink I quite into the mire.
There is comfort that deceives,
  Joy that by my mischance lives,
  Helpers there who only grieve me,
  Friends who only mock and leave me.
Nothing in the world endureth,
  Or the soul's thirst can allay;
  Fleeting is the rank that lureth.
  Have I riches? What are they
[7]
Better than small dust of earth?
  Have I pleasure? What's it worth?
  What to-day my heart doth gladden,
  That to-morrow doth not sadden?
Comfort, joy, in boundless measure,
  Stor'd, Lord Jesus, are in Thee,
  Pastures of unfading pleasure,
  Where we roam and feast so free.
Light of joy! illumine me
  Ere my heart quite broken be!
  Jesus, let mine eyes behold Thee;
  Lord, refresh me and uphold me!
Heart, rejoice, for He doth hear thee,
  And He visits thee again;
  Now thy Saviour draweth near thee,
  Bid Him gladsome welcome then,
And prepare thee for thy guest,
  Enter thou into His rest,
  While with open heart receiving,
  Tell Him all that is thee grieving.
[8]
Lo! the things that seem'd to hinder
  How they all fall out for good.
  Hark! how He in accents tender
  Comforts thee in gracious mood.
Ceas'd the dragon has to roar,
  Scheming, raging, now no more.
  His advantages forsake him,
  He must to th' abyss betake him.
Now thy life is calm and even,
  All thy heart's desire is thine;
  Christ Himself to thee hath given
  All He hath—exhaustless mine!
His grace is thy fairest crown,
  Thou His seat art and His throne;
  With Himself as one He makes thee,
  Freely to His bosom takes thee.
God His golden-curtain'd Heaven
  Spreadeth to encompass thee!
  Lest thou shouldst away be driven
  By thy raging enemy.
[9]
Angel hosts keep watch and ward
  At thy side and are thy guard;
  Lest in journeys aught should hurt thee,
  By the way their arms support thee.
All the ill thou hast done ever
  It is now remitted quite;
  God's love thee doth now deliver
  From sin's tyrant pow'r and might.
Christ the Prince hath won the day,
  Rise against thee what ill may,
  He, to purest good converting,
  Robbeth of the pow'r of hurting.
All for thine advantage proveth,
  E'en what hurtful may appear.
  Christ accepteth thee and loveth,
  And His thoughts are all sincere.
Thou in turn but faithful be,
  Then shall certainly by thee,
  With the angel hosts in Heaven,
  Thanks and praise for aye be given.
[10]

SAY WITH WHAT SALUTATIONS?

Say with what salutations
  Shall I Thine advent greet?
  Desire of all the nations,
  My Joy and Succour meet!
O Jesus! Jesus! lead me
  On by Thy blessèd light;
  What's Thy delight thus guide me
  To understand aright.
With palms doth Zion meet Thee,
  Spreads branches in the way;
  To raise my soul to greet Thee
  Glad psalms I'll sing to-day.
My heart shall blossom ever,
  O'erflow with praises new,
  And from Thy name shall never
  Withhold the honour due.
What hast Thou e'er neglected
  For my good here below?
  When heart and soul dejected,
  Were sunk in deepest woe,
[11]
When from Thy presence hidden,
  Where peace and pleasure are,
  Thou camest, and hast bidden
  Me joy again, my Star!
In bitter bondage lying,
  Thou com'st and sett'st me free;
  'Neath scorn and shame when sighing,
  Thou com'st and raisest me.
Thy grace high honour gives me,
  Abundance doth bestow,
  That wastes not, nor deceives me
  As earthly riches do.
No other impulse led Thee
  To leave Thy throne above,
  Upon Thine errand sped Thee,
  But world-embracing love!
A love that deeply feeleth
  The wants and woes of men,
  No tongue its fulness telleth,
  It passeth human ken.
[12]
In thy heart be this written,
  Thou much afflicted band!
  Who evermore art smitten
  With griefs on every hand.
Fear not! let nothing grieve thee,
  For help is at thy door,
  He'll consolation give thee,
  Oil in thy wounds will pour.
No care nor effort either
  Is needed day and night,
  How thou may'st draw Him hither
  In thine own strength and might.
He comes, He comes with gladness!
  O'erflows with love to thee,
  To chase away the sadness
  He knows oppresseth thee.
Sin's debt, the mighty burden
  Let not thy heart affright;
  The Lord will freely pardon,
  His grace will cover quite.
[13]
He comes! He comes! Salvation
  Proclaiming everywhere,
  Secures His chosen nation
  Their heritage so fair!
Thy foes why should they move thee?
  Their wiles and rage are vain,
  Thy Saviour, who doth love thee,
  Will scatter them again.
He comes! a Conq'ror glorious,
  He'll scatter every band
  Of foes—His course victorious
  Too few they're to withstand.

He comes to judge each nation;
   Who curs'd Him, curse shall He;
   With grace and consolation,
   Who lov'd, receiv'd shall be.
Oh! come, Thou Sun, and lead us
   To everlasting light,
   Up to Thy mansions guide us
   Of glory and delight.

Birth of Christ.—Christmas.

[14]

OF THE APPEARANCE OF THE ANGELS.

Behold! behold! what wonder's here!
   The gloomy night turns bright and clear,
   A brilliant light dispels the shade,
   The stars before it pale and fade.
A wondrous light it is, I trow,
   And not the ancient sun shines now,
   For, contrary to nature, night
   Is turned by it to day so bright.
What means He to announce to us,
   Who nature's course can alter thus?
   A mighty work design'd must be
   When such a mighty sign we see.
To us vouchsafèd can it be
   The Sun of Righteousness to see,
   The Star from Jacob's stem so bright,
   The woman's Seed, the Gentiles' Light?

[15]

'Tis even so—for from the sky
   Heav'n's hosts with joyful tidings hie,
   That He is born in Bethl'hem's stall,
   Who Saviour is and Lord of all!
Oh blessedness! the goodly throng
   Of sainted fathers waited long
   To see this day, with hope deferr'd,
   As we may learn from God's own word.
Awake, ye sons of men, awake!
   Up! up! and now your journey take
   With me, let us together go
   To where the blessèd angels show.
Behold! there in yon gloomy stall
   He lies who ruleth over all;
   Where once their food the cattle sought,
   The Virgin's child for rest is brought.
Oh, child of Adam! ponder well,
   And stumble not at what I tell,
   He who appears in this low state
   For us is, and aye shall be great.

[16]

In mortal flesh we Him behold,
   Who all things made and doth uphold,
   The Word who was with God is He,
   Himself is God whom now we see.
It is God's sole-begotten Son
   Through whom we now approach His throne,
   The First and Last, the Prince of Peace,
   The Conqueror through whom wars cease.
The times predicted are fulfill'd,
   God's fiery wrath must now be still'd;
   His Son, made man, doth bear our load
   Of guilt, our peace buys with His blood.
It is a time of joy to-day,
   With mourning and with woe away!
   Woe, woe to him who us revil'd!
   God's seen in flesh—we're reconcil'd.
The Lord who bears our sin is here,
   Who'll bruise the serpent's head is near,
   The Death of death—the Woe of hell—
   The Lord of Life with us doth dwell.

[17]

All foes are put our feet beneath,
   For sin and Satan, hell and death,
   Are brought to shame and put to flight
   Upon this great, this wondrous night.
Oh! happy world, thrice happy they!
   Who on this lowly infant stay
   Their souls, and with believing eyes
   In Him their Saviour recognize.
Now praise the Lord whoe'er can praise,
   Who from their low estate to raise
   His enemies, from His high throne
   Sent down His lov'd, His only Son.
Up! join the angel host and cry,
   Now glory be to God most High;
   Let peace prevail the world around,
   Good-will to men and joy abound.

[18]

NOW WITH JOY MY HEART IS BOUNDING.

Now with joy my heart is bounding,
   With delight
   Angels bright
   Praises forth are sounding.
Hark! hark! how the choirs of Heaven,
   Through the sky
   Raise the cry,
   Christ to you is given!
He who's mighty to deliver,
   Goes that He
   Earth may free
   From all woes for ever.
God is man, man to deliver,
   His dear Son
   Now is one
   With our blood for ever.
God in us must now take pleasure,
   For He gives
   Whom He loves
   Far beyond all measure.

[19]

To redeem us He hath given
   His own Son
   From the throne
   Of His might in Heaven.
Who Himself and Kingdom ever,
   Giveth free,
   Oh! could He
   Drive us from Him?—never!
Will not God's own Son now bless us?
   He who loves
   And removes
   All things that distress us!
Had our human nature ever
   By the Lord
   Been abhorr'd,
   He had been man never.
Had our Lord delighted ever
   In our grief,
   He relief
   Would have brought us never.

[20]

All transgression He assumeth,
   That we've done
   'Neath the sun,
   And our Lamb becometh.
As our Lamb His life is given,
   So that we,
   From death free,
   May have peace and Heaven!
Now He's in the manger lying,
   Me and thee
   Calleth He,
   In sweet accents crying,
"Banish, brethren, what's distressing,

All your ills,
All that falls,
I bring times of blessing."
Come, and let us now go thither,
Let us all,
Great and small.
Flock in crowds together.
[21]
Love Him who with deep love burneth,
See the light
He so bright
Kindly on us turneth.
Ye who sink in deepest anguish,
Look ye here,
Joy is near,
Grieve no more, nor languish.
Cleave to Him and He will bring you
To the place,
By His grace,
Where no pain will wring you.
All ye hearts, oppress'd with sorrow,
Ye who feel
Sin's sore ill
And conviction's arrow,
Courage now! for One is living
Who hath skill
You to heal,
All your pain relieving.
[22]
All ye poor ones and distressèd,
Come—come ye
Take—'tis free,
Of His store so blessèd.
Here do all good gifts flow over,
Here is gold
Stores untold!
Here your hearts recover!
Gracious Saviour! deign to hear me,
And let me
Hang on thee,
Undisturb'd stay near Thee.
Of my life Thou art the Giver,
I through Thee
Joyfully
Live contented ever.
Guilt no longer can distress me,
Son of God!
Thou my load
Bearest to release me.
[23]
Stain in me Thou findest never,
I am clean,
All my sin
Is remov'd for ever.
For Thy sake I'm clean all over,

Thou dost me
Graciously
With fair raiment cover.
To my heart's throne I will raise thee,
Glory mine!
Flow'r divine!
Let me love and praise Thee.
Diligently I'll preserve Thee,
To the skies
To Thee rise,
Here live for and serve Thee.
With Thee I at last shall wander,
Joyfully,
Endlessly,
And in glory yonder!
[24]

A CAROL.

Come, and Christ the Lord be praising,
 Heart and mind to Him be raising,
 Celebrate His love amazing,
 Worthy folk of Christendom!
Sin, death, hell, may all be grieving,
 Satan shame feel to him cleaving,
 We salvation free receiving,
 Cast our every care away.
See what God for us provideth,
 Life that in His Son abideth,
 And our weary steps He guideth
 From earth's woe to heav'nly joy.
His soul deeply for us feeleth,
 He His love to us revealeth,
 He who in the heavens dwelleth
 Came to save us from our foe.
[25]
Jacob's star His advent maketh,
 Soothes the longing heart that acheth,
 And the serpent's head He breaketh,
 Scattering the pow'r of hell.
Op'd hath He and freedom gain'd us
 From the prison that contain'd us,
 Where much grief and sorrow pain'd
us,
 And our hearts were bow'd with woe.
O bless'd hour when we receivèd
 From the foe who us deceivèd
 Liberty, when we believèd,
 And Thee, gracious Savior, prais'd.
Beauteous Infant in the manger,
 O befriend us! beyond danger
 Bring us where is turn'd God's anger,
 Where with angel hosts we'll praise!
[26]

AT THE MANGER.

Thy manger is

My paradise,
O Jesus Christ!
Where feeds my soul delighted.
There 'fore mine eyes
The Word now lies,
Who to our flesh
In person is united.
Whom wind and sea
 Obey, e'en He
 In servant's form
 And place for men's appearing.
God's own Son, Thou
 Assumest now
 Clay weak and mean,
 Such as our own, art wearing!
Thou, highest Good!
 Dost raise our blood
 Up to Thy throne,
[27]
High o'er all heights whatever!
 Pow'r endless, Thou
 Art brother now
 To us who like
 The grass and flowers, wither!
What harm can do
 Our soul's dread foe
 To us at all,
 Though full of gall his spirit?
The things that he
 Accuseth me
 And others of,
 From Adam we inherit.
Be silent, fiend!
 There sits my Friend,
 My flesh and blood,
 High in the heav'ns enthronèd:
What Thou dost smite
 The Prince of might
 From Jacob's stem
 With honours high hath ownèd.
[28]
His health and light,
 Heal and give sight,
 And heaven's Joy
 All earthly ill undoeth.
Immanuel,
 Of joy the Well,
 The devil, hell,
 And all their pow'r subdueth.
Believing heart,
 Whoe'er thou art,
 Be of good cheer,
 Let nothing e'er depress thee;
Because God's Son
 Makes thee God's own,

God must prove true
  To thee, and ever bless thee.
Now think and see
  How gloriously,
  He over all
[29]
Distress hath thee uplifted.
  He who reigns o'er
  The angels, more
Than thou art, is
With blessedness not gifted.
Lo! seest thou
  Before thee now,
  Thy flesh and blood,
Who air and clouds rules ever.
What can there be
(I ask of thee)
That can arise,
To fear thee to deliver?
Things oft affright
  Thy feeble sight
  And make thee sigh,
Thy consolations vanish:
Come hither, then,
Behold again
Christ's manger here,
And all misgivings banish.
[30]
Though plagued with care,
  Yet ne'er despair!
  Thy Brother ne'er
Thy misery disdaineth;
His gracious heart
Feels every smart,
Nor when He sees
Our woe, from tears refraineth.
To Him now go,
  He'll help bestow
  And rest, and thou
Good cause shalt have for blessing.
Full well He knows
What burns and glows,
What on the heart
Of each sick one is pressing.
He therefore bore
  The wrath so sore
  Of the dread cross
[31]
In His flesh, shrinking never,
  That through His pain
  He might retain
The memory
Of our distresses ever.
The gate is He
  That leadeth me

To present joy,
And to eternal blessing.
He soon doth send
  A happy end
  To all the grief
On pious heart that's pressing.
The world's base pelf
  Leave to itself,
  And make thou sure,
This treasure thine remaineth.
It firmly keep
Nor let it slip,
It there a crown
For soul and body gaineth!
[32]

BESIDE THE MANGER.
Now at the manger here I stand,
  My Jesus, Life from Heaven!
  I stand, and bring Thee in my hand
What Thou to me hast given.
Take it, it is my mind and wit,
Heart, soul, and all I have, take it,
And deign to let it please Thee!
With Thy great love beyond compare,
  My soul Thou fillest ever,
  Thy glance so sweet, Thine image fair,
My heart forgetteth never.
How otherwise e'er could it be,
How could I ever banish Thee,
From my heart's throne, O Saviour!
Ere ever I began to be,
  Thou hadst for me appearèd,
  And as Thine own hadst chosen me
Ere Thee I knew or fearèd.
[33]
Before I by Thy hand was made,
  Thou hadst the plan in order laid,
  How Thou Thyself shouldst give me.
I lay still in death's deepest night,
  Till Thou, my Sun, arising,
  Didst bring joy, pleasure, life, and light,
My waken'd soul surprising.
O Sun! who dost so graciously
Faith's goodly light to dawn in me
Aye cause; Thy beams how beauteous!
With rapture do I gaze on Thee,
  Ne'er can enough adore Thee,
  Pow'r more to do is not in me,
I'll praise and bow before Thee.
Oh! that my mind were an abyss,
My soul a sea, wide, bottomless,
That so I might embrace Thee.

Oh! let me kiss that mouth of Thine,
  My Jesus, Saviour gracious!
  Thy mouth that e'en the sweetest wine,
And milk and honey precious,
[34]
In pow'r and virtue doth excel,
  Of comfort, strength, and sap 'tis full,
  And inwardly refreshes.
When oft my heart within doth cry,
  No comfort can discover,
  It calls to me, Thy friend am I,
Thine ev'ry sin I cover;
My flesh and bone, why mournest thou?
Let thy heart be of good cheer now,
Thy debt, I have discharg'd it.
Who is the Master, where is he,
  Who in perfection sketcheth
  The hands this infant dear to me
Now smilingly outstretcheth?
The snow is clear, and milk is white,
But both lose all their value quite
Before these hands so beauteous.
Oh! wisdom fails me utterly
  For honouring and praising
  The eyes this infant fixedly
To mine is ever raising.
[35]
The fall moon, it is clear and fair,
  The golden stars most beauteous are,
  But these eyes far excel them.
Oh! that a star so passing fair
  Should in a crib be holden!
  Who mighty nobles' children are
Should lie in cradles golden!
Ah! hay and straw too wretched are,
Silk, velvet, purple better far,
Were for Thee, Child! to lie on.
Remove the straw, remove the hay,
  From where the child reposes,
  And flow'rs I'll bring that lie He may
On violets and roses.
With tulips, pinks, and rosemary,
From goodly gardens pluck'd by me,
I'll from above bestrew Him.
And snow-white lilies here and there
  His side shall be thrown over;
  When closed His eyes with slumber are,
Them shall they softly cover.
[36]
But Thou mayest love the grass so dry,
  My Child! more than the things that I
  Have spoken or have thought of.

Not for the world's pride dost Thou care,
  Nor joys the flesh doth offer;
  In human form Thou liest there,
  For us to do and suffer,
  Seek'st joy and comfort for my soul,
  While waves of trouble o'er Thee roll;
  I never will Thee hinder.
One thing I hope Thou'lt grant to me,
  My Saviour! ne'er deny me,
  That I may evermore have Thee
  Within, and on, and by me.
  And let my heart Thy cradle be,
  Come, come and lie Thou down in me,
  With all Thy joys and treasures!
'Tis true, that I should think how poor
  And mean my entertaining,
  Than dust and ashes I'm no more,
  Thou mad'st, art all-sustaining,
[37]
Yet Thou'rt a guest belov'd and priz'd,
  For never yet hast Thou despis'd
  Him who delights to see Thee!

IMMANUEL! TO THEE WE SING.

Immanuel! to Thee we sing,
  The Fount of life, of grace the Spring,
  Than fairest lily fairer far,
  Lord of all Lords, the morning Star!
  Hallelujah!
With all Thy people, Lord, we raise
  To Thee our heart-felt songs of praise,
  That Thou, O long-expected Guest!
  Hast brought us our desirèd rest.
  Hallelujah!
Since the Creator said—"Light be!"
  How many a heart hath watch'd for Thee!
  Of Fathers, Prophets, Saints the throng
  With ardent hope have waited long.
  Hallelujah!
[38]
Than others more, the Shepherd King
  Belov'd by Thee, and wont to sing
  Thy praise on sounding harp, inspir'd
  By deeper longing, Thee desir'd.
  Hallelujah!
Ah Zion! that thy Lord to thee
  Would come and set thy captives free;
  Ah! that our help would now arise
  And gladden Jacob's waiting eyes.
  Hallelujah!
There art Thou now, Thou ever-bless'd!
  There dost Thou in the manger rest;
  The world Thou deck'st, all things hast made—
  Thou'rt naked there, in weakness laid.
  Hallelujah!
A stranger art Thou here below,
  To whom the Heav'ns allegiance owe;
  A mother's milk dost not despise,
  Who art the Joy of angels' eyes.
  Hallelujah!
[39]
The bounds of ocean fix'd hast Thou,
  Who art a swaddled infant now;
  Thou'rt God—a bed of straw Thou hast.
  Thou'rt man—yet art the First and Last.
  Hallelujah!
Of every joy Thou art the spring,
  Yet sorrow oft Thy heart doth wring.
  The Gentiles' Light and Hope Thou art,
  Yet findest none to soothe Thy heart.
  Hallelujah!
The sweetest Friend of man Thou art,
  Though many hate Thee in their heart!
  The heart of Herod loathèd Thee,
  Yet what art Thou? Salvation free!
  Hallelujah!
Thy meanest servant, Lord! am I,
  I say it in sincerity;
  I love Thee, but not half so well
  As I should love,—more love I'd feel.
  Hallelujah!
[40]
My pow'r is weak, though will be there,
  But my poor heart against Thee ne'er
  Shall rise t' oppose,—Thou wilt receive
  By grace the little I can give.
  Hallelujah!
Thou to be weak dost not disdain,
  Dost choose the things the world deems vain,
  Art poor and needy, and dost come,
  By love impell'd, to want's drear home!
  Hallelujah!
Thou sleepest on the lap of earth,
  The manger where Thou at Thy birth
  Wast laid to rest, the hay, the stall
  Were mean, were miserable all.
  Hallelujah!
And therefore doth my courage rise,
  Thy servant wilt Thou not despise;
  The gracious mind that dwells in Thee
  Fills me with hope and gladdens me.
  Hallelujah!
[41]
Lord! though I've pass'd in sin my days,
  And wandered far from wisdom's ways,
  Yet therefore Thou to earth hast come,
  To bring the wand'ring sinner home.
  Hallelujah!
Had I no debt of sin to face,
  How could I ever share Thy grace?
  In vain for me Thine advent here,
  Had I no wrath of God to fear.
  Hallelujah!
Lord, fearlessly I come to Thee,
  Thou keep'st my soul from anguish free;
  Thou bear'st the wrath, dost death destroy,
  And sorrow turnest into joy.
  Hallelujah!
My Head Thou art, Thy member I
  In turn am, and Thy property;
  Lord, I will serve Thee while I live
  With all the grace Thou deign'st to give.
  Hallelujah!
[42]
Loud hallelujahs here I'll sing,
  With joy that from my heart doth spring,
  And when I reach yon mansions fair
  I will repeat them ever there.
  Hallelujah!
[43]

New Year.

OF THE CIRCUMCISION OF CHRIST.

Why should they such pain e'er give Thee,
  Why inflict such cruel smart?
  Jesus, why should they so grieve Thee,
  Who're uncircumcis'd in heart,

By this rite? Though Thou art free
   From the law's yoke utterly,
   Yet man's nature art Thou wearing,
   But no sin its beauty marring.
For Thyself Thou dost not bear it,
   Of the Cov'nant Thou art Head;
   'Tis our debts that make Thee share it,
   That like grievous load of lead
Lie upon us, and Thy heart
   Pierce e'en to the inmost part;
   These Thou bearest to deliver
   Us, who could have paid them never.
[44]
Let your hearts be glad, ye debtors!
   Let the world rejoice to-day,
   For the Son of God our fetters
   Breaks, the price begins to pay.
This day is the Law fulfill'd,
This day is God's anger still'd,
   Whom to death law did deliver,
   God's Son makes God's heirs for ever.
We this grace enough can never
   Own, nor for it grateful be;
   Heart and mouth, O Saviour! ever
   Shall exalt and honour Thee!
We shall praise with all our pow'r
   All Thy goodness, Thee adore,
   While in weakness here we wander,
   And Thy praise re-echo yonder!
[45]

SONG.

In pray'r your voices raise ye
   To God, and Him now praise ye,
   Who to our life from heaven
   All needed strength hath given.
The stream of years is flowing,
   And we are onward going,
   From old to new surviving,
   And by His mercy thriving.
In woe we often languish,
   And pass through times of anguish,
   When fearful war aboundeth,
   That earth itself surroundeth.
As faithful mother keepeth
   Guard while her infant sleepeth,
   And all its grief assuageth
   When angry tempest rageth;
[46]
So God His children shieldeth,
   Them full protection yieldeth;
   When need and woe distress them,
   His loving arms caress them.
In vain is all our doing,
   The labour we're pursuing
   In our hands prospers never,
   Unless God watcheth ever.
Our song to Thee ascendeth,
   Who every day defendeth
   Us, and whose arm averteth
   The pain our hearts that hurteth.
O God of mercy! hear us;
   Our Father! be Thou near us;
   'Mid crosses and in sadness
   Be Thou our Spring of gladness.
To me and all be given,
   Who from the heart have striven
   To gain Thy benediction,
   Hearts patient in affliction.
[47]
Oh! close the gates of sorrow,
   And by a glorious morrow
   Of peace, may places sadden'd
   By bloodshed dire be gladden'd.
With richest blessings crown us,
   In all our ways, Lord! own us;
   Give grace, who grace bestowest
   To all, e'en to the lowest.
Of all forlorn be Father,
   All erring ones ingather,
   And of the poor and needy
   Be Thou the succour speedy.
Grace show to all afflicted,
   And to all souls dejected,
   By melancholy haunted,
   May happy thoughts be granted.
All earthly gifts excelling,
   The Holy Ghost indwelling,
   Give us to make us glorious,
   And lead to Thee victorious.
[48]
All this Thy hand bestoweth,
   Thou Life! whence our life floweth,
   Thus Thou Thy people meetest
   With New Year's blessing greetest.

The Sufferings of Christ.--Good Friday.
[49]

A LAMB BEARS ALL THE GUILT AWAY.

Isa. liii. 4-7; John i. 29.

A Lamb bears all its guilt away
   The world thus to deliver,
   All sins of sinners patiently
   It bears and murmurs never.
It goes, and weak and sick is made
An off'ring on the altar laid,
   All pleasure it forsaketh,
   Submits to shame, and scorn, and wrath,
To anguish, wounds, stripes, cross, and death,
   This cup with gladness taketh.
This Lamb, He is the soul's great Friend
   And everlasting Saviour,
   God chooseth Him sin's reign to end
   And bring us to His favour.
[50]
"Go forth, my Son! redeem to Thee
   The children who're exposed by me
   To punishment and anger.
The punishment is great, and dread
The wrath, but Thou Thy blood shalt shed,
   And free them thus from danger."
"I'll go where, Father! thou dost send,
   Bear what on me Thou layest,
   My will doth on Thy word depend,
   My work is what Thou sayest."
O mighty love! O wondrous love!
Thou canst do all our thoughts above,
   Make God His Son deliver!
O love! O love! Thy pow'r how great!
Thou did'st Him e'en to death prostrate
   Whose glance the rocks can shiver.
Thou martyr'st Him upon the tree,
   With spear and nails destroying
   Thou slay'st Him, lamblike, ruthlessly,
   Till heart and veins are flowing,
[51]
The heart with many a long-drawn sigh,
   And till His veins are copiously
   Their noble life-blood yielding.
Sweet Lamb! what shall I do for Thee
   For all the good Thou doest me,
   Thus saving me and shielding?
All my life long I'll cleave to Thee
   And shall forget Thee never,
   As always Thou embracest me
   I will embrace Thee ever.
My heart's Light Thou shalt ever be,
   And when my heart shall break in me
   Thy heart shall fail me never.
O Thou, my Glory, I to Thee
   Myself as Thine own property
   Herewith resign for ever!
I ever shall both night and day
   Thy loveliness be singing,
   An offering of joy shall aye
   Myself to Thee be bringing.

[52]
My stream of life shall still to Thee,
   And to Thy name, outpourèd be,
     In gratitude enduring.
   Of every good Thou doest me,
   My soul shall mindful strive to be,
     In memory securing!
Shrine of my heart! now open'd be,
   To thee shall now be given
   Fair treasures that far greater be
     Than earth, and sea, and heaven.
   Away! gold of Arabia,
   Myrrh, calamus, and cassia,
     Far better I discover!
   My priceless treasure is, O Thou
   My Jesus! what so freely now
     From Thy wounds floweth over!
Good use of this behoves it me
   At all times to be making,
   My shield in conflict shall it be,
     My joy when heart is breaking,
[53]
In happiness my song of joy;
   When all things else my taste do cloy,
   This manna then shall feed me,
   In thirst my well-spring shall it be,
   In solitude converse with me,
     And out and in shall lead me!
What can death's poison do to me?
   Thy blood to me life giveth,
   And when the sun burns fervently,
     With grateful shade relieveth;
   And when with sorrow sore oppress'd
   I ever find in it my rest,
     As sick men on their pillows.
My anchor art Thou, when my skies
   Are clouded o'er, and tempests rise,
     My bark 'whelm in the billows.
And when at last heav'n's gate I see,
   And taste the kingdom's pleasure,
   This blood shall then my purple be,
     I'll clothe me in this treasure;
[54]
It shall be then my glorious crown,
   In which I'll stand before the throne
     Of God, with none to blame me;
   And as a bride in fair array,
   I'll stand beside my Lord that day,
     Who woo'd, and then will claim me.

SEE, WORLD! THY LIFE ASSAILED.

See, world! thy Life assailèd;
   On the accurs'd tree nailèd,
     Thy Saviour sinks in death!
The mighty Prince from Heaven
   Himself hath freely given
     To shame, and blows, and cruel wrath!
Come hither now and ponder,
   'Twill fill thy soul with wonder,
     Blood streams from every pore.
Through grief whose depth none knoweth,
   From His great heart there floweth
     Sigh after sigh of anguish o'er!
[55]
Who is it that afflicts Thee?
   My Saviour, what dejects Thee,
     And causeth all Thy woe?
Sin Thou committed'st never,
   As we and our seed ever,
     Of deeds of evil nought dost know.
I many times transgressing,
   In number far surpassing
     The sand upon the coast,
I thus the cause have given,
   That Thou with grief art riven,
     And the afflicted martyr host.
I've done it, and deliver
   Me hand and foot for ever
     Thou justly might'st to hell.
The mock'ry to Thee offer'd,
   The scourging Thou hast suffer'd,
     My soul it was deserv'd it well.
The load Thou takest on Thee,
   That press'd so sorely on me,
[56]
Than stone more heavily.
   A curse, Lord, Thou becamest,
   Thus blessings for me claimest,
     Thy pain must all my comfort be.
Not death itself Thou fearest,
   As surety Thou appearest
     For all my debts and me.
For me Thy brow is crownèd
   With thorns, and Thou'rt disownèd
     By men, and bear'st all patiently.
Into death's jaws Thou springest,
   Deliv'rance to me bringest
     From such a monster dire.
My death away Thou takest,
   Thy grave its grave Thou makest;
     Of love, O unexampled fire!
I'm bound, my Saviour, ever,
   By ties most sacred never
     Thy service to forsake;
With soul and body ever,
   With all my pow'rs t' endeavour,
     In praise and service joy to take.
[57]
Not much can I be giving
   In this poor life I'm living,
     But one thing do I say:
   Thy death and sorrows ever,
   Till soul from body sever,
     My heart remember shall for aye.
Before mine eyes I'll place them,
   And joyfully embrace them,
     Wherever I may be,
   They'll be a glass revealing
   Pure innocence, and sealing
     Love and unfeign'd sincerity.
Of sin how great the danger,
   How it excites God's anger,
   How doth His vengeance burn
   How sternly He chastiseth,
   How His wrath's flood ariseth,
     Shall I from all Thy suff'rings learn.
From them shall I be learning,
   How I may be adorning,
[58]
My heart with quietness,
   And how I still should love them
   Whose malice aye doth move them
     To grieve me by their wickedness.
When tongues of bad men grieve me,
   Of peace and name deprive me,
     My restive heart I'll still;
   Their evil deeds enduring,
   Of pardon free assuring
     My neighbour for his ev'ry ill.
I'll on the cross unite me
   To Thee, what doth delight me
     I'll there renounce for aye.
Whate'er Thy Spirit's grieving,
   There I'll for aye be leaving,
     As much as in my strength doth lay.
Thy groaning and Thy sighing,
   Thy thousand tears and crying,
     That once were heard from Thee,
   They'll lead me to Thy glory,
   Where I shall joy before Thee,
     And evermore at rest shall be!
[59]

TO THE COUNTENANCE OF THE LORD JESUS.

Oh! bleeding head, and wounded,
   And full of pain and scorn,
   In mockery surrounded
     With cruel crown of thorn!
Oh Head! before adornèd
   With grace and majesty,
   Insulted now and scornèd,
     All hail I bid to Thee!

They spit upon and jeer Thee,
   Thou noble countenance!
   Though mighty worlds shall fear Thee,
   And flee before Thy glance.
How hath Thy colour faded,
   The light too of Thine eye!
   Say who to pale hath made it?
   None shone so brilliantly.
Now from Thy cheeks is vanish'd
   Their colour once so fair;
   From Thy red lips is banish'd
   The splendour that was there.
[60]
Death's might hath all things taken,
   Hath robb'd Thee ruthlessly;
   Thy frame, of strength forsaken,
   Doth hence in weakness lie.
O Lord! it was my burden
   That brought this woe on Thee,
   I earn'd it—for my pardon
   It has been borne by Thee.
A child of wrath, look on me,
   Turn not away Thy face;
   O Saviour! deign to own me,
   And smile on me in grace.
My Guardian, now confess me,
   My Shepherd, me receive!
   Thou evermore dost bless me,
   All good things dost Thou give.
Thy mouth hath often given
   Me milk and sweetest food.
   And many a taste of Heaven
   Thy Spirit hath bestow'd.
[61]
Oh! do not, Lord, deride me,
   I will not hence depart,
   Here will I stand beside Thee,
   When breaks Thine anguish'd heart;
When on Thy breast is sinking
   In death's last fatal grasp
   Thy head, e'en then unshrinking
   Thee in mine arms I'll clasp.
Nought ever so much blesses,
   So much rejoices me,
   As when in Thy distresses
   I share a part with Thee.
My Life, ah! were it ever
   Vouchsaf'd me on Thy cross
   My soul up to deliver,
   How blessèd were my loss!
Thanks from my heart I offer
   Thee, Jesus, dearest Friend,
   For all that Thou didst suffer,
   My good didst Thou intend.

[62]
Ah! grant that I may ever
   To Thy truth faithful be,
   And in the last death-shiver
   May I be found in Thee.
When hence I must betake me,
   And death at last must meet,
   Lord, do not then forsake me,
   Thy child with welcome greet.
When terror has bereft me,
   Of heart and hope, again,
   Lord! from my woe uplift me,
   In virtue of Thy pain.
Be Thou my consolation
   When death o'ertaketh me;
   May Thy death-tribulation
   Before mine eyes then be!
I'll on Thee, fondly gazing,
   Fix my believing eyes,
   While firmly Thee embracing,—
   He dies well who so dies.
[63]

THE SEVEN WORDS SPOKEN BY THE LORD JESUS ON THE CROSS.

My heart! the seven words hear now
   That Jesus Christ hath spoken,
   When on the cross His heart through woe
   And murder dire was broken;
   Ope now the shrine,
   And lock them in,
   As gifts all price excelling.
   In bitter grief,
   They'll give relief,
   'Neath crosses joy instilling.
His first and chiefest care He made
   Who hated Him to cover:
   God for the wicked men He pray'd,
   That He'd their sin look over.
   "Forgive, forgive,"
   He said in love,
   "Them every one, O Father!
   Not one doth see
   What doeth he,
   In ignorance 'tis rather!"
[64]
How fair it is, let all learn here,
   To love their foes who grieve them,
   And all their faults with hearts sincere
   Aye freely to forgive them.
   He also shows,
   How grace o'erflows
   His heart, how kind His mood is,

   That e'en his foe,
   Who'd work Him woe,
   Doth in Him find what good is!
Then to His mother doth He speak,
   Who stood near him He loveth,
   And as He can, though voice be weak,
   With words of comfort sootheth:
   "Woman! there see
   Thy son, for me
   Thou shalt by him be guarded.
   Disciple! see,
   Let her by thee
   As mother be regarded."
[65]
O faithful heart! thou car'st for all
   Thine own who truly love Thee,
   When they in tribulation fall
   Thou seest, the sight doth move Thee;
   A friend in need,
   In word and deed,
   Thou at their side appearest,
   Dost by Thy grace
   Find them a place,
   Them to good souls endearest.
The third thing that Thy lips have said
   Thou spak'st to him beside Thee,
   When, "Think upon me then," he pray'd,
   "When God Himself shall guide Thee
   Up to Thy throne,
   Thy head shall crown
   As Lord of earth and heaven:"
   "To walk with Me
   To-day shall thee
   In Paradise be given."
[66]
O blessèd word! O voice of joy!
   Can aught affright us?—never!
   Let death who seeketh to destroy,
   Now disappear for ever!
   Though he rage sore,
   What can he more
   Than soul and body sever?
   And meanwhile I
   Mount up on high,
   In joy to dwell for ever.
Christ's word gives deepest peace and joy,
   The robber's trouble stilleth;
   But He cries from the agony
   His holy breast that filleth,
   "Eli, my God,
   What heavy load

Am I, Thy Son, now bearing?
I call, and Thou
Art silent now,
Though I sink, seem'st not caring."
[67]
This lesson learn, thou child of faith,
  When God His count'nance veileth,
Lest thou be cast down in the path
  When trouble thee assaileth:
Firm to Him cleave,
Though He may leave,
He'll comfort soon, and cheer thee;
True do thou be,
Cry mightily,
Until He turn and hear thee.
The Lord His voice now clear doth raise
  Through thirst that paineth sorely;
"I thirst," the Spring eternal says,
  The Lord of life and glory.
What meaneth He?
He showeth thee
How He thy load sinks under,
That thou did'st pile
For Him, the while
In sin's ways thou did'st wander.
[68]
Thereby He also telleth thee
  How much He longs that ever
His cross in each may fruitful be,
  Fail of its end may never.
Mark this all ye,
Now carefully,
Who're in soul tribulation:
Th' eternal Sun
Refuseth none
The soul's part and salvation.
And as the gloomy night of death
  Upon the Lord descended,
"'Tis finish'd," He with dying breath
  Said, "now my work is ended;
What was foretold
In days of old,
By seers who went before me,
Doth now betide;
I'm crucified,
And men now triumph o'er me."
[69]
"'Tis finish'd!"—why then toilest thou?
  In vain thy labour ever!
As if aught human strength can do,
  Could e'er from guilt deliver!
'Tis done! beware,
And never dare
To add aught to it ever;
Do thou believe,
In faith aye cleave
To Him, forsake Him never.
His voice at length the Lord doth raise,
  High over all 'tis swelling:
"My spirit, Father! to the place
  Take where Thou'rt ever dwelling,
My soul receive,
That now doth leave
This body sorely riven."
And at the word,
To the great Lord
Release from pain was given.
[70]
Oh! would to God, that I might end
  My life as His was ended,
My spirit unto God commend
  As His was then commended.
O Christ, my Lord!
May Thy last word
The last be by me spoken;
So happily
I'll go to Thee,
When life's last thread is broken.
[71]

Resurrection of Christ.—Easter.

UP! UP! MY HEART WITH GLADNESS.

Up! up! my heart with gladness,
  See what to-day is done!
How after gloom and sadness
  Comes forth the glorious Sun!
My Saviour there was laid
Where our bed must be made,
When to the realms of light
Our spirit wings its flight.
They in the grave did sink Him,
  The foe held jubilee;
Before he can bethink him,
  Lo! Christ again is free.
And victory He cries,
And waving tow'rds the skies
His banner, while the field
Is by the Hero held!
[72]
Upon the grave is standing
  The Hero looking round;
The foe, no more withstanding,
  His weapons on the ground
Throws down, his hellish pow'r
To Christ must he give o'er,
And to the Victor's bands
Must yield his feet and hands.
A sight it is to gladden
  And fill the heart with glee,
No more affright or sadden
  Shall aught, or take from me
My trust or fortitude,
Or any precious good
The Saviour bought for me
In sov'reign love and free.
Hell and its bands can never
  Hurt e'en a single hair,
Sin can I mock at ever,
  Safe am I everywhere.
[73]
The mighty pow'r of death
  Is my regard beneath;
It is a pow'rless form,
  Howe'er it rage and storm.
The world my laughter ever
  Moves, though it rage amain,
It rages, but can never
  Do ill, its work is vain.
No trouble troubles me,
My heart from care is free,
Misfortune is my prize,
The night my fair sunrise.
I cleave, and cleave shall ever,
  To Christ, a member true,
Shall part from my Head never,
  Whate'er He passes through;
He treads the world beneath
His feet, and conquers death
And hell, and breaks sin's thrall;
I'm with Him through it all.
[74]
To halls of heav'nly splendour
  With Him I penetrate;
And trouble ne'er may hinder
  Nor make me hesitate.
What will, may angry be,
My Head accepteth me,
My Saviour is my Shield,
By Him all rage is still'd.
He to the gates me leadeth
  Of yon fair realms of light,
Whereon the pilgrim readeth,
  In golden letters bright:
"Who's there despised with me,
Here with me crown'd shall be;
Who there with me shall die,
Here's raised with me on high!"
[75]

BE JOYFUL ALL, BOTH FAR AND NEAR.

Be joyful all, both far and near,
  Who lost were and dejected:
To-day the Lord of glory here,
  Whom God Himself elected

As our Redeemer, who His blood
    Upon the cross shed for our good,
    Hath from the grave arisen.
How well succeeded hath thy might,
    Thou foe of life so ruthless!
    To kill the Lord of life and light;
    Thine arrow through Him scathless
    Hath pass'd, thou base injurious foe!
    Thou thought'st when thou hadst laid Him low,
    He'd lie in dust for ever.
No, no! on high His head is borne,
    His mighty pow'r asunder
    Thy gates hath burst, thy bands hath torn,
    Thyself hath trodden under
[76]
His feet; who doth in Him confide
    Thy pow'r and claims may now deride
    And say, "Thy sting, where is it?"
Thy pow'r is gone, 'tis broken quite,
    And it can hurt him never
    Who to this Prince with all his might
    With heart and soul cleaves ever,
    Who speaks with joy, "I live, and ye
    Shall also live for aye with me,
    For I this life have purchas'd.
"The reign and pow'r of death are o'er,
    He never need affright you;
    I am his Lord, the Prince of pow'r,
    And this may well delight you;
    And as your risen Head I live:
    So ye, if ye on me believe,
    Shall be my members ever.
"Of hell have I the overthrow
    Accomplish'd, none now needeth
    To fear the pains of endless woe,
    Who Me and My word heedeth;
[77]
He's freed from Satan's grievous yoke,
    Whose head I bruis'd, whose might I broke,
    And he can never harm him."
Now prais'd be God, who vict'ry hath
    To us through Jesus given,
    Who peace for war, and life for death,
    With entrance into heaven,
    Hath purchas'd, who death, sin, and woe,
    World, devil, what our overthrow
    Would seek, for aye hath vanquish'd.

Whitsuntide.

[78]

O FATHER! SEND THY SPIRIT DOWN.

O Father! send Thy Spirit down,
    Whom we are bidden by Thy Son
    To seek, from Thy high heaven;
    We ask as He taught us to pray,
    And let us ne'er unheard away
    From 'fore Thy throne be driven.
No mortal man upon the earth
    Is of this gift so noble worth,
    No merit we've to gain it;
    Here only grace availeth aught,
    That Jesus Christ for us hath bought,
    His tears and death obtain it.
O Father! much it grieves Thy mind
    Us in such woful plight to find,
    As Adam's fall hath brought us;
    The evil spirit's pow'r, this fall
    Hath brought on him, and on us all,
    But Christ to save hath sought us.
[79]
To our salvation, Lord, we cleave,
    That we are Thine in Christ believe,
    From Him nought shall us sever;
    And through His death and precious blood,
    Our mansions fair, and highest good,
    We look for, doubting never.
This is a work of grace indeed,
    The Holy Spirit's strength we need,
    Our pow'r is unavailing;
    Our faith and our sincerity
    Would soon, O Lord! in ashes lie,
    Were not Thy help unfailing.
Of faith Thy Spirit keeps the light,
    Though all the world against us fight,
    And storm with every weapon.
    Although the prince of this world too,
    May take the field to lay us low,
    No ill through him can happen.
The Spirit's is the winning side,
    And where He helps, the battle's tide
[80]
Assuredly abateth.
    What's Satan's might and majesty?
    It falleth when His standard high
    The Spirit elevateth.
The chains of hell He rends in twain,
    Consoles and frees the heart again
    From everything that grieveth;
    And when misfortunes o'er us low'r
    He shields us better in their hour,
    Than ever heart conceiveth.
The bitter cross He maketh sweet,
    In gloom His light our eyes doth greet,
    Care of His sheep He taketh,
    Holds over us the shield, and when
    Night falls upon His flock, He then
    To rest in peace us maketh.
The Spirit God gives from above
    Directeth all who truly love
    In ways of safety ever;
    He guides our goings every day,
    From paths of bliss to turn away
    Our feet permits us never.
[81]
He maketh fit, and furnishes
    With needed gifts for service those
    Who here God's house are rearing,
    Adorns their minds and mouths and hearts,
    And light to them for us imparts,
    What's dark to us thus clearing.
Our hearts He opens secretly
    When they His word so faithfully
    As precious seed are sowing;
    He giveth pow'r to it, where'er
    It takes root, tending it with care,
    And waters it when growing.
He teacheth us the fear of God,
    Loves purity, makes His abode
    The soul that sin refuseth;
    Who contrite are, virtue revere,
    Repent, and turn to Him in fear
    And love, He ever chooseth.
He's true, and true doth aye abide,
    In death's dark hour He's at our side,
[82]
When all from us recedeth;
    He sootheth our last agony,
    Up to the halls of bliss on high
    In joy and trust He leadeth.
Oh! happy are the souls and bless'd,
    Who while on earth permit this Guest
    To make in them His dwelling;
    Who now receive Him joyfully,
    He'll take up to God's house on high,
    Their souls with rapture filling.
Now, Father, who all good dost give,
    Our pray'r hear, may we all receive
    From Thee this priceless blessing;
    Thy Spirit give, that here He may
    Rule us, and there in endless day
    Our souls be aye refreshing.

Repentance.

[83]

CONSOLATION FOR PENITENCE.

Let not such a thought e'er pain thee,
    As that thou art cast away,
But within God's word restrain thee,
    That far otherwise doth say.
E'en though thou unrighteous art,
True and faithful is God's heart.
Hast thou death deserv'd for ever?
God's appeas'd, despond thou never!
Thou art, as is every other,
    Tainted by the poison, sin,
That the serpent, and our father,
    Adam, by the fall brought in.
But if thou God's voice dost hear,
    "Turn to me, do good," ne'er fear,
Be of good cheer, He thy yearning
Will regard, thy pray'r ne'er spurning.
[84]
He is not a bear nor lion
    Thirsting only for thy blood,
Faithful is thy God in Zion,
    Gentle ever is His mood.
God aye as a Father feels,
He's afflicted by our ills,
Our misfortune sorrow gives Him,
And our dying ever grieves Him.
"Truly," saith He, "as I'm living,
    I the death of none desire,
But that men themselves upgiving,
    May be rescu'd from sin's mire."
When a prodigal returns,
God's heart then with rapture burns,
Wills that not the least one even
Ever from His flock be driven.
Shepherd was so faithful never,
    Seeking sheep that go astray;
Couldest thou God's heart see ever,
    How He cares for them alway,
[85]
How it thirsts and sighs and burns
    After him who from Him turns,
From His people's midst doth wander,
    Love would make thee weep and ponder.
God the good not only loveth
    Who in His house ever dwell,
But His heart compassion moveth
    Tow'rds those whom the prince of hell
Hath enslav'd, the cruel foe
Who men's hearts with hate to glow
Makes 'gainst Him, who when He ever
Moves His foot, can make earth quiver.
Deep His love is and enduring,
    His desire is ever great,
He is calling and alluring
    Us to enter heav'n's wide gate.
When they come, whoe'er they be,
Seeking now that liberty
From the devil's fangs be given,
Glad are all the hosts of heaven.
[86]
God and all on high who're dwelling,
    'Fore whom heav'n must hush its voice,
When their Maker's praise forthtelling,
    O'er our penitence rejoice;
But what has been done amiss
Cover'd now and buried is,
All offence to Him we've given,
All, yea all, is now forgiven.
From no lake so much is gushing,
    No depth is so deep at all,
With such force no stream is rushing,
    All compar'd with God is small;
Nought is like His grace so great,
That remits our mighty debt,
That He ever throweth over
All our lives e'en as a cover.
Soul, why art thou sad and dreary?
    Rest now and contented be!
Why wilt thou thyself so weary
    When there is no need for thee?
[87]
Though thy sins appear to thee
    Like a vast and shoreless sea,
If thou with God's heart compare them,
    'Twill a trifle seem to bear them.
Could we myriad worlds discover
    All sunk in apostacy,
Had the sins there o'er and over
    Every one been done by thee,
Oh! still they were less by far
Than the light of grace so clear
Could on earth extinguish ever,
God from greater could deliver.
Of such wondrous love and favour
    Open wide the door to me;
Ey'rywhere and aye, my Saviour,
    Tasted be Thy grace by me.
Love me, Lord! and let me be
Nearer ever drawn to Thee,
That I may embrace and love Thee,
Never more to anger move Thee!
[88]

FOR THEE, LORD, PANTS MY LONGING HEART.—PSALM XXV.

For Thee, Lord, pants my longing heart,
    My hope and confidence Thou art;
    My hope can never shaken be,
    Nor e'er be put to shame by Thee.
Whoe'er he be that scorns Thy name,
    And turns from Thee, shall come to shame;
    But he who ever lives to Thee,
    And loves Thee, shall untroubled be.
Accept my soul, O Lord! by grace,
    And keep me right in all my ways,
    And let Thy truth illumine me
    Along the path that leads to Thee.
Thou art my only light below,
    No other helper here I know;
    I wait on Thee both night and day,
    Why dost Thou, then, O Lord, delay?
[89]
Ah, Lord! now turn Thine eyes away
    From paths where I have gone astray;
    Of my ill ways what thinkest Thou,
    That I've pursued from youth till now?
Remember, Thou my Guardian Lord!
    Thy loving-kindness and sweet word,
    Whereby Thou giv'st them comfort sweet
    Who lay themselves low at Thy feet.
Who prove themselves, and sin confess,
    The Lord in mercy rich will bless;
    Who keep His testimonies all,
    The Lord will hold them when they fall.
The heart that with the Lord is right
    In grief He'll gladden with His light,
    When sunk in need, weigh'd down by loss,
    Shall triumph e'en beneath the cross.
Ah! Lord, full well thou knowest me,
    My spirit lives and moves in Thee;
    Thou seest how my bleeding heart
    Longs for the help Thou canst impart.
[90]
The griefs that now my heart oppress,
    The griefs my heavy sighs express
    Are great and sore, but Thou art He
    To whom nought e'er too great can be.
To Thee I therefore raise mine eyes,
    To Thee mine ardent longings rise—

Ah! let Thine eye now rest on me
  As Thou wast wont, Lord, graciously.
And when I need supporting grace,
  Turn not away from me Thy face;
  May what Thou deignest to impart
  Of my desires be counterpart.
The world is false, it acts a part,
  Thou art my Friend, sincere in heart;
  Man's smile is only on his mouth,
  Thou lovest us in deed and truth.
Foil Thou the foe, his nets all tear,
  And baffle every wile and snare;
  When all with me once more is well,
  May gratitude my bosom swell.
[91]
Still may I in Thy fear abide,
  And go right on nor turn aside;
  Give single aim that honours Thee,
  Smarts rather than a burden be.
Rule, Lord, and bring me unto Thee,
  And other saints along with me;
  Remove whate'er of ill dost find,
  Renew and cleanse each heart and mind.
Wash Thou away each sinful stain,
  Deliver from all grief and pain,
  And lead us soon by heav'nly grace
  To realms of endless joy and peace.
[92]

SONG OF REPENTANCE FROM PSALM CXLIII.

Lord, lend a gracious ear
  To my desire sincere,
  From heart all free from guile,
  And glad me with Thy smile,
  Accept my petition.
Not wealth is my request,
  That on the earth doth rest,
  That shall at length decay,
  With earth must pass away,
  And can never save us.
The treasure I desire
  Is Thine own grace, O Sire!
  The grace that Thy dear Son,
  Of saving grace the throne,
  By His death hath purchas'd.
Thou pure and righteous art,
  Unholy is my heart,
  All dead in sin I live,
  But sin dost Thou forgive,
  Who art God most faithful.
[93]
And be Thy faithfulness
  My trust and happiness;
  Turn from my sin Thy face
With overflowing grace
  My guiltiness cover.
Consider what we be—
  A moment, where are we?
  As brittle as frail glass,
  As fading as the grass,
  By a breath we're swept off.
If Thou wilt only view
  The evil that we do,
  So great our load of sin,
  None e'er could stand within
  Heaven's gate most holy.
How Jesus Christ for me
  Himself hath giv'n, see!
  What I to do have fail'd
  His power hath avail'd,
  His doing and dying.
[94]
Thou lov'st remorse and smart,
  Behold, here is a heart
  That knows and feels its sin,
  And burns like fire within
  With grief, pain, and sorrow.
I'm like a thirsty land
  From which Thy gracious hand
  Hath long withheld the rain,
  Until we seek in vain
  For strength, fruit, or moisture.
Like hart upon the heath,
  That cries with gasping breath
  For water fresh and clear,
  I call into Thine ear,
  Fount of living water!
My spirit, Lord, revive,
  Rich consolation give;
  Speak, that my soul may rest
  Upon the friendly breast
  Of Thy love eternal.
[95]
Give me a trustful mood,
  That when the mighty flood
  Of sin o'erwhelmeth me,
  My grief absorb'd may be
  In Thy mercy's ocean.
Drive off the wicked foe
  That seeks my overthrow;
  Thou art my Shepherd, I
  Will be eternally
  A sheep of Thy pasture.
As long as I shall dwell
  On earth, to do Thy will
  I give myself to Thee,
  And evermore shall be
  Thine own faithful servant.
Though feeble, I shall be
  Still grateful unto Thee,
  For in Thy might alone,
  That worketh in Thine own,
  All my power standeth.
[96]
Then send Thy Spirit down,
  Who points out to Thine own
  The way that pleaseth Thee;
  They never mov'd shall be,
  Who keep Him indwelling.
Thou shalt go on before,
  Shalt open me the door
  That leads to wisdom's way,
  I'll follow every day,
  Copying Thee ever.
And when at length 'tis giv'n
  To tread the courts of heav'n,
  With angel hosts to Thee
  I'll sing eternally
  To Thy praise and glory.

Prayer and the Christian Life.
[97]

FOR WISDOM.

O God! from Thee doth wisdom flow,
  All I can do Thou well dost know;
  If Thine own grace doth not sustain,
  Then all my labour is in vain.
As shapen in iniquity,
  No good by nature can I see;
  My heart can never serve Thee right,
  In folly it is sunken quite.
Yea, Saviour! I'm too mean and small
  To treat Thy law and claims at all;
  What for my neighbour's good may be,
  Is hid from and unknown to me,
My life is very short and weak,
  A thread, a passing wind may break;
  The splendour that the world doth prize
  Is vain and worthless in mine eyes.
[98]
If earth with all its gifts would dow'r,
  And give me honour, fame, and pow'r,
  And did I not enjoy Thy light,
  Then were I nought, 'twere deepest night.
What use, though much we've learnèd here,
  If first we do not learn Thy fear,
  And ne'er to serve Thee right attain?
  It is more loss to us than gain.
The knowledge men themselves attain

May easily mislead again;
  And when our art hath done its best,
  On all sides obstacles arrest.
How many ruin now the soul
  Through craft, as did Ahithophel,
  And come, through ignorance of Thee,
  And through their wit, to misery.
O God, my Father! lend an ear,
  My supplication deign to hear;
  Far from me may such folly be;
  A better mind, Lord! give to me.
[99]
Give me the Wisdom from above
  Thou giv'st to all who truly love,
  The wisdom that before Thy throne
  For ever shineth in their crown.
I love her lovely face so bright,
  She is my joy and heart's delight,
  The fairest is that holdeth me,
  Mine eyes she pleaseth wondrously.
She's noble, and of rarest worth,
  From Thee, Most High! derives her birth;
  She's like the Monarch of the day,
  Rich gifts and virtues her array.
Her words are sweet and comfort well,
  When grief our eyes with tears doth fill;
  When 'neath affliction's rod we smart,
  'Tis she revives the drooping heart.
She's full of grace and majesty,
  Preserves us from mortality;
  Who earnestly to get her strives,
  E'en when he's dying, still he lives.
[100]
She's the Creator's counsellor,
  In deeds and words excels in pow'r;
  Through her the blind world knows and sees
  What God in heav'n above decrees.
What mortal knows His Maker's mind?
  Who is he that could ever find
  The counsel out God hath decreed,
  The way wherein He'd have us tread?
The soul upon the earth doth live,
  Its heavy burdens sorely grieve,
  The faculties distracted be,
  From error here are not set free.
What God doth who can e'er explore,
  And say what He rejoiceth o'er?
  Unless Thou who dost ever live
  Dost Thine own wisdom to us give.
Then send her from Thy heav'nly throne,
  And give her to Thine handmaid's son;
  Her bountifully, Lord! impart
  To the poor dwelling of my heart.
[101]
Command her to abide with me,
  And my companion aye to be;
  Whene'er I labour, may she e'er
  Me help my heavy load to bear.
May I be taught by her wise hand
  To know and rightly understand
  That I to Thee alone may cleave,
  According to Thy will may live.
And give to me ability,
  To truth may I still open be,
  That sour of sweet I never make,
  Nor darkness for the light may take.
To Thy word give desire and love,
  And true to duty may I prove;
  To pious souls join'd may I be,
  Take counsel with them constantly.
And may I gladly every man,
  By deed and counsel when I can,
  To guide and succour ready be,
  In truth and in sincerity.
[102]
So that in ev'rything I do,
  In Thy love I may ever grow;
  For who to wisdom doth not give
  Himself, unlov'd by Thee must live.

FOR SUCCESS AND BLESSING IN ALL CHRISTIAN WORKS AND PURPOSES.

My God! my works and all I do,
  Rest only on Thy will, I know,
  Thy blessing prospers ever,
  When Thou dost guide, we persevere
  In right ways, erring never.
It standeth not in human might
  That man's devices issue right,
  His way with gladness endeth:
  God's counsel only prospers sure,
  'Tis He success who sendeth.
[103]
Man often thinks in haughty mood
  That this or that is for his good,
  Yet widely he mistaketh;
  He often thinketh that is ill
  Whereof the Lord choice maketh.
But wise men e'en who joyfully
  Begin a good work, frequently
  Reach no good termination;
  They build a castle firm and strong,
  But sand is the foundation.
How many in their fancy stray
  High over mountain peaks away,
  Ere they bethink them ever;
  Down to the ground they fall, and vain
  Has been their strong endeavour.
Dear Father! therefore, who the crown
  And sceptre bear'st on Heav'n's throne,
  Who from the clouds dost lighten,
  Regard my words, and hear my cry,
  From Thy seat my soul brighten!
[104]
Vouchsafe to me the noble light
  That from Thy countenance so bright
  On pious souls aye breaketh,
  And where the pow'r of wisdom true
  Through Thine own pow'r awaketh.
Give understanding from on high,
  That I henceforward may rely
  Upon mine own will never.
  Be Thou my counsel, that I may
  Fulfil the good, Lord! ever.
Prove all things well, whate'er is good
  Give to me, but what flesh and blood
  Doth choose, withhold it ever.
  The highest good, the fairest part,
  Thy glory is and favour.
Sun of my soul! my chief delight!
  Whate'er is pleasing in Thy sight,
  Oh! may I choose and do it;
  And what's displeasing unto Thee,
  May I, O Lord! eschew it.
[105]
Is it from Thee? my work then bless;
  Is it of man? withhold success,
  And change what I'm resolving.
  Dost Thou not work? 'twill come to nought,
  In failure soon involving.
But should Thine and our enemy
  Begin to rage revengefully
  Against the good Thou'rt meaning,
  My comfort is, Thou canst avert
  His wrath, me ever screening.
Draw near, and let it easy be,
  What seems impossible to me,
  A happy issue give it;
  What Thou Thyself didst undertake,
  Thy wisdom did conceive it.
Though hard at first the work may be,
  And I may through the deepest sea
  Of bitter grief be passing,
  Oh! may I only driven be
  To sighs and pray'r unceasing.

[106]
Whoever prays and trusteth Thee,
   With valiant heart shall victor be
   O'er all that frightens ever,
   In thousand pieces speedily
   Grief's heavy stone shall shiver.
The way to good is almost wild,
   With thorns and hedges is it fill'd;
   Along this way who goeth
   He by the Spirit's grace at last
   What heav'nly joy is knoweth.
I am Thy child, my Father Thou!
   Thou hast abundance to bestow,
   Nought can I find within me;
   Help, that I may maintain my ground,
   As victor home, Lord! bring me.
Thine be the glory and the pow'r!
   Thy mighty works I'll more and more
   From heart with rapture swelling,
   Before Thy folk and all the world,
   All my life long be telling.
[107]

TWOFOLD, FATHER! IS MY PRAYER.—PROV. XXX. 7-9.

Twofold, Father! is my pray'r,
   Twofold the desire I there
   Lay before Thee, who dost give
   What's good for us to receive;
   Grant the pray'r that Thou dost know,
   Ere my soul to Thee must go
   From the body's bands below.
Grant that far from me may be
   Lying and idolatry;
   Poverty immoderate
   Give me not, nor riches great;
   Too great wealth or poverty
   Is not good, for either may
   'Neath the devil's pow'r us lay.
Give to me, my Saviour! give
   Modest portion while I live;
   Evermore supply my need,
   Giving me my daily bread;
   Little, with contented mood,
   And a conscience pure and good,
   Is the best can be bestow'd.
[108]
If my cup should overflow,
   Proud in spirit I might grow,
   Thee deny with scornful word,
   Asking who is God and Lord?
   For the heart with pride doth swell,
   Often knows not when 'tis well,
   How itself enough t' extol.
Should I bare and naked be,
   Sunk in too deep poverty,
   Faithless, I might wickedly
   Steal my neighbour's property;
   Force might use and artifice,
   Follow lawless practices,
   Never ask what Christian is.
God! my Treasure and my Light,
   Neither course for me were right,
   Either would dishonour Thee,
   Sink me into hell's dark sea;
   Therefore, give, Lord! graciously,
   What Thy heart designs for me,
   Moderate my portion be!
[109]

SIRACH'S PRAYER FOR A HAPPY AND TEMPERATE LIFE.

Creator, Father, Prince of might!
   Who life to me art giving,
   Unless Thou guid'st my life aright
   In vain here am I living.
   For while I'm living, I am dead,
   To sin devoted ever;
   Whose life in mire of sin is led,
   The true life he hath never
   Beheld one moment even.
Then turn on Thy poor child Thy face,
   In darkness do not leave me;
   That I may shun sin and disgrace,
   Good counsel ever give me!
   To keep my lips a guard, Lord, send,
   May no word ever leave them
   That e'er Thy people could offend
   Let nought I say e'er grieve them,
   Nor ever Thee dishonour!
[110]
Forbid, Father! that mine ear
   Upon this earth so evil,
   Against Thy name and pow'r should hear
   The wicked rage and cavil.
   Let not the poison and the gall
   Of slanderers defile me;
   If I such filth should touch at all
   It surely would beguile me,
   Might e'en quite overthrow me.
Lord, keep mine eyes, control their glance,
   May they work evil never;
   A bold and shameless countenance
   Keep Thou far from me ever!
   What's honest, keeps due boundaries,
   What angels seek in heaven,
   What is well-pleasing in Thine eyes,
   For it by me be striven,
   All luxury disdaining.
Oh! may I ne'er delighted be
   By revelling and eating;
   Be what Thou lov'st belov'd by me,
   Though others shun it, hating.
[111]
The lusts wherein the flesh doth roll,
   To hell will draw us ever;
   The joys the world doth love, the soul
   And spirit will deliver
   To torment everlasting.
Oh! happy he who eats heav'n's bread,
   And heav'nly water drinketh,
   Who tastes nought else, nought else doth heed,
   Nought else desires, and thinketh
   Of that alone which strength can bring,
   The life we'll live for ever
   With God, and with the hosts who sing
   His praise, in joy that never
   Shall know an interruption.
[112]

FOR CONSTANT CHRISTIAN FRIENDSHIP.

Jesus! Thou, my dearest Brother,
   Who dost well to me intend,
   Thou mine Anchor, Mast, and Rudder,
   And my truest Bosom-Friend.
   To Thee, ere was earth or heaven,
   Had the race of man been given;
   Thou, e'en me, poor guest of earth,
   Chosen hadst before my birth.
Thou art free from guile, Lord! ever
   Innocent of all that's base;
   But on this sad earth whenever
   I in meditation gaze,
   There I find deception living;
   Who excelleth in deceiving,
   Who the best dissemble can,
   He's the best and wisest man.
Hollow and unfaithful ever
   Is the friendship of the earth;
   Seemeth she a man to favour?
   'Tis but for the gold he's worth;
[113]
Are we prosp'rous, do we flourish?
   She will smile on us, and nourish;
   Doth misfortune o'er us low'r?
   She forsakes us in that hour.
Drive away from me, and shield me
   From such instability;
   If I, Father, have defil'd me
   (For I also human be)
   With this mire, and did I ever

Falsehood love, oh! now deliver.
All my guilt I own to Thee,
Patience give, and grace to me!
May I ne'er be overtaken
By the evils Thou hast said
Come on those who've truth forsaken,
And with wares deceptive trade;
For Thou sayest Thou disownest,
As abomination shunnest,
Ev'ry hypocrite's false mood,
Who talks, but doth not the good.
[114]
May my heart be constant ever,
Faithful still to every friend;
When to grief Thou dost deliver
Them, and 'neath the cross they bend,
May I even then ne'er shun them,
But like unto Thee, Lord, own them,
Who, when we were poor and bare,
Tended'st us with fondest care.
After Thy will, Saviour, give me
One in whom I may confide,
Who will faithful counsel give me
When my heart is sorely tried;
To whom I may freely utter
All I feel, with nought to fetter,
In the measure I may need,
'Till my heart from care is freed.
Oh! let David's bliss betide me,
Give to me a Jonathan
Who will come and stand beside me
Like a rock, though every man
[115]
From my company should sever,
Who his heart will give me ever,
Who'll stand firm in every hour,
When sun shines or tempests low'r.
Out of all the men who're living,
Choose me a believing friend,
Who to Thee is firmly cleaving,
On Thine arm doth aye depend;
Who may by Thy will relieve me,
Help and comfort ever give me,
Help, from sympathizing heart,
Comfort, when I feel grief's smart.
When 'tis only the mouth loveth,
Then the love is ill bestow'd;
Whose love but to good words moveth
While he keeps a hateful mood,
Whom self-interest rules ever,
Who when honey falls, stays never,
But escapeth speedily,—
Ever far be such from me!

[116]
In my weakness and my sinning,
Move my friend to speak to me,
By his words of kindness winning,
Never as an enemy.
Who reproves in love and sadness
Is like him, in days of gladness,
Who pours balsam over me
That by Jordan floweth free.
Riches great were I possessing,
Priceless were my property;
Jesus! did Thy hand such blessing
Graciously bestow on me,
Were such friend, Lord! ever near me,
By His constancy to cheer me;
Who doth honour Thee, and fear
He hath such a treasure near.
Good friends like to staves are ever,
Whereon men lean as they go,
That the weak one can deliver,
When he slides and lieth low:
[117]
Sad his case who such ne'er knoweth,
Who through life all friendless goeth,
Weary is his lonely way,
When he falls, to help who stay?
Gracious Saviour! let it please Thee,
Be my Friend in every hour,
Be my Friend, till death release me,
Be my faithful Staff of pow'r!
When Thou to Thyself wilt bind me,
Then a heart Thou soon wilt find me,
By Thy Holy Spirit fir'd
With good thoughts to me inspir'd.

FOR TEMPORAL AND ETERNAL WELFARE.

O God, my Father! thanks to Thee
I bring with deep humility,
That Thou Thine anger endest,
And that Thy Son,
Our Joy and Crown,
Into the world Thou sendest.
[118]
He hath appear'd, His precious blood
Hath pourèd forth in such a flood,
That all our sins it washes.
Who to Him cleaves,
He soon relieves
Of burdens, and refreshes.
I come, Lord! as the best I may,
Take me into the band, I pray,
Of those who are forgiven,
Who through this blood
Are just and good,
And shall be bless'd in heaven.
Oh! let mine eye and hand of faith
This noble pledge keep without scath,
Away from me ne'er casting;
And let this light
Lead me aright,
To the light everlasting.
The mansion of my soul prepare,
Cast out whate'er is evil there,
[119]
And build in me Thy dwelling:
Thy grace so free
Reveal to me,
My soul with Thy love filling.
All things are mine when I have Thee,
Thou void of gifts canst never be;
A thousand ways Thou knowest
On earth to keep
Thy feeble sheep;
Enough Thou aye bestowest.
Grant that I in my station here
Thee in Thy word may ever fear,
So guide what things concern me,
That found in me
True faith may be,
And may with truth adorn me.
And give me a contented mind,
For when with godliness combin'd,
Great gain thence ever floweth.
Then what of good
It pleaseth God
To give, great peace bestoweth.
[120]
The little that by God's great grace
The righteous as his portion has,
To honour more commendeth,
Than all the gold
The world doth hold,
And with proud spirit spendeth.
The faithful, Lord, to Thee are known,
Thou art their Joy, and they Thine own,
To shame thou putt'st them never;
Comes scarcity,
Their bread from Thee
They find in all lands ever.
God loveth him who fears and cleaves
To Him, sees that no mischance grieves,
In his ways joyeth ever;
And if he slide,
God doth abide,
Doth bless him and deliver.
God's eye is upon all who wait
And hope in Him both soon and late,

[121]
In all need to deliver,
  E'en in the hour
  When to devour
  Death threatens them for ever.
Lord, Thou canst only gracious be,
  Thou givest all to know and see
  Thy goodness and Thy favour,
  Who with their mouth
  And heart in truth
  Own Thee their only Saviour.
Make Her Thy care especially,
  Whom Thou as monarch hast rais'd high
  This land and nation over;
  With rest and peace
  The land, Lord! bless,
  The throne with blessings cover.
Preserve, Lord! our dear native land
  In Thine embrace and mighty hand;
[122]
Protect us all together
  From error's voice,
  From enemies,
  From fire and plague deliver.
All whom I love, keep every day,
  Let all the hosts of hell away
  From young and old be driven!
  Here, may we be
  In time by Thee
  Preserv'd, and there in heaven!
For obvious reasons the original has been slightly altered. The German is,
Insonderheit nimm wohl in acht
  Den Fürsten, &c.

FOR THE LOVE OF CHRIST.

O Jesus Christ! my fairest Light,
  Who in Thy soul dost love me,
  I ne'er can tell it, nor its height
  Mete, 'tis so high above me,
  Grant that my heart may warm to Thee,
  With ardent love ne'er ceasing,
  Thee embracing,
  And as Thy property,
  Cleave to Thee, ever gazing.
[123]
Grant that an idol in me may
  Dwell e'en a moment never,
  Grant me to make Thy love, I pray,
  My crown and prize for ever!
  Cast all things out, take all away,
  That Thee and me would sever,
  So that ever
  By Thy love, my pow'rs may
  Be kindled, and cool never!
How friendly, blessèd, sweet, and fair
  Is Thy love, Jesus ever!
  While this remains, distress and care
  Can grieve my spirit never.
  Then let me only think of Thee,
  Be seeing, hearing, feeling,
  Loving, telling
  Of Thee, and Thy great love to me
  Oh! be Thou more revealing!
Oh! that this greatest, highest good,
  I might for aye be tasting!
  Oh! that in me this noble blood
  Might glow to everlasting!
[124]
Help me to watch, Lord! day and night,
  This blessèd treasure shielding
  From unyielding
  Foes, who 'gainst us the might
  Of Satan's realm are wielding!
My Saviour! Thou in love to me
  Hast down to death descended,
  And like a murd'rer on the tree
  And thief hast been suspended,
  Spit on, despis'd and wounded sore,
  The wounds which Thee have riven,
  May it even
  To me at the heart's core
  With love to feel be given.
The blood that hath been shed by Thee
  Is good and precious ever,
  My heart is wicked desp'rately,
  Hard as a millstone nether.
[125]
Ah! let the virtue of Thy blood
  My flinty heart be bending,
  Entrance finding;
  And may Thy love, life's flood
  Through all my veins be sending.
Oh! were my heart op'd to receive
  The blood-drops that were falling
  From Thee, wrung by my sin that eve
  In agony appalling!
  Oh! that the fountains of mine eyes
  Were op'd, and with much sighing,
  And sore crying,
  Gush'd forth, as tears and sighs
  Of men in love who're dying.
Oh! that I as a little child
  With weeping eyes might trace Thee,
  E'en till Thy heart with love was fill'd
  And Thine arms did embrace me.
[126]
And until Thou Thy heart to me
  With sweet love flowing over,
  Should'st discover,
  And we united be,
  Thy goodness for my cover.
Ah! draw me, Saviour! after Thee,
  And so shall I be hasting,
  I run, and in my heart shall be
  Thy love with rapture tasting;
  The gracious words from Thee I'll hear
  Sweet comfort shall give ever;
  Me deliver
  From sin, and every fear,
  These shall o'ercome me never.
My Comfort, Treasure, Health, and Light,
  My Life and Saviour tender!
  Ah! take me for Thy portion quite
  As I myself surrender!
[127]
There's nought but pain apart from Thee,
  I nought but gall discover,
  Earth all over,
  Nought ever comforts me,
  No balm can me recover.
But Thou the Rest most blessed art,
  In Thee are joys eternal.
  Grant, Jesus! grant that my poor heart
  Feed in Thy pastures vernal!
  Be Thou the flame that burns in me,
  My Balsam, ease that giveth,
  And relieveth
  Pain that here constantly
  Makes me heave sighs, and grieveth.
Ah! fairest one, what faileth me
  In Thy great love, of blessing?
  It is my sun that lightens me,
  My well-spring, me refreshing!
[128]
My sweetest wine, my heav'nly bread,
  My cov'ring when before Thee,
  And my glory,
  My shield in hour of need,
  My house that riseth o'er me!
Ah! dearest love, why was I born,
  If Thou my soul forsakest?
  If Thou withdraw'st, I'm all forlorn,
  All good from me Thou takest.
  O may I seek Thee as my guest,
  With all my best endeavour
  Keep Thee ever;
  And when I Thee arrest,
  Let Thee go from me never.
I've been belov'd by Thee for aye,

To follow Thou did'st move me;
  Before I good could e'er essay,
  E'en then did Thy heart love me:
[129]
Ah! noble Rock! Thy love below
  May it for ever guide me,
  And beside me
  Be it where'er I go,
  To aid whate'er betide me.
And may Thy love adorn my place,
  Where'er my lot Thou'rt casting;
  And if I wander from Thy ways,
  To bring me back be hasting.
  And let me ever counsel wise,
  Good works from Thee be learning,
  From sin turning,
  And when from falls I rise,
  Come back to Thee with yearning!
And ever be my joy in woe,
  When weak, with Thy strength stay me;
  And when my course is run below,
  I down to rest will lay me.
[130]
Then may Thy love and truth with me,
  O Christ! abide for ever,
  Leave me never,
  Till I Thy glory see,
  Oh! may they waft me thither!

THE FIRST PSALM OF DAVID.

Bless'd is he who never taketh
  Counsel of ungodly men!
  Bless'd, the right who ne'er forsaketh,
  Nor in sinners' paths is seen,
  Who the scorners' friendship spurns,
  From their seats away who turns,
  Who delight in God's word taketh,
  This his meditation maketh.
Bless'd is he who pleasure taketh
  In God's laws' most perfect way,
  It is his lov'd resort who maketh
  Where he lingers night and day!
[131]
Oh! His blessing blooms and grows,
  As the palm where water flows,
  And abroad its branches spreadeth,
  And the wayworn pilgrim shadeth.
He will truly ever flourish
  Who God's word delights to do,
  Air and earth alike will nourish
  Him, till ripe his fruit shall grow.
Though his leaf grow old, yet he
  Ever fresh and green shall be,
  God success to his endeavour
  Giveth, and it prospers ever.
But he who in sin's ways goeth
  Is like chaff the wind before,
  When it riseth up and bloweth,
  And we find it here no more.
Where the Lord His people guide,
  There the godless ne'er abide,
  God the faithful loves and guideth,
  On the wicked wrath abideth.
[132]

THE 112TH PSALM OF DAVID.

Bless'd is he the Lord who loveth,
  At His word doth tremble aye!
  Bless'd whose heart him freely moveth
  God's commandments to obey.
Who the Highest loves and fears,
  Findeth increase with the years
  Of all that to him is given
  By the bounteous hand of Heaven.
His dear children shall stand ever
  Like to roses in their blow;
  Flowing with God's goodness over,
  On his generations go.
What the body needs below
  God who rules all will bestow,
  He will bounteously relieve them,
  Plenty in their dwellings give them.
The right deeds of the believer
  Nought can shake, they stand secure;
  If a storm o'ertakes him ever,
  Still doth God, his Light endure,
[133]
Comforts, shieldeth with His pow'r,
  So that after darkness' hour,
  After night of tears and sorrow,
  Joy and sunshine glad the morrow.
God's compassion, grace, and favour
  For the faithful still endure.
  Blessèd are the souls who ever
  Think upon the needy poor,
Love them, seek to do them good;
  For the ever-living God
  In His arms of grace will bear them,
  And a home above prepare them.
When the black clouds o'er them lighten,
  And the pealing thunders shock,
  They shall sit, and nought shall frighten,
  Like the dove hid in the rock;
They'll remain eternally,
  And their memory shall be
  Upon every side extending,
  As their branches trees are sending.
[134]
When misfortunes overtake them,
  Whereby sinners low are laid,
  Firm their courage, nought can shake them,
  And their hearts are undismay'd;
Undismay'd, from care are free,
  Hearts that unreservedly
  To the Lord their God are given,
  Love Him when forsaken even.
Who delight take in relieving
  Sad ones, to the Lord are dear;
  What the loving hands are giving,
  God will recompense e'en here.
Who much giveth much will gain,
  He shall not desire in vain,
  What his heart desires and willeth,
  God in His good time fulfilleth.
But the foes who triumph'd o'er them,
  They shall see depart beneath;
  Satan who such malice bore them,
  Evermore shall gnash his teeth:
[135]
Sorely will it him displease
  When their blessedness he sees,
  Yet that he can rob them never,
  Only waste himself for ever.

THE 121ST PSALM OF DAVID.

Lord! to Thee alone I raise
  Evermore mine eager eyes,
  Upturn'd is my constant gaze
  To the hills that pierce the skies:
To the hills whence flow to me
  Help and saving health from Thee!
All my succour comes to me
  From my great Creator's hand,
  Who hath deck'd so beauteously
  Earth and sky, air, sea, and land,
  And with ev'ry good supplied,
  That our needs be satisfied.
[136]
Lest thy feet, my soul! should stray
  From the narrow path of right,
  He is with thee in the way,
  And preserves thee day and night.
Trust Him! and the hosts of hell
  Never more shall work thee ill.
Sleepless vigils doth He keep
  When thou liest down to rest;
  When thou'rt sunk in slumbers deep,
  To thy side at His behest
  Angel hosts then wing their flight,
  Thee to guard through all the night.
All thou hast and all thou art
  Is encircled by His love;

Ev'ry grief that wrings thy heart
  Doth He graciously remove.
Soul and body shieldeth He,
  When dark tempests threaten thee.
When the noonday's burning sun
  All thy body's strength doth blight,
When the midnight stars and moon
  Dazzle with their brilliant light,
[137]
Then His hand of mighty pow'r,
  Shades thee in the trying hour.
May He still protection yield,
  Faithful Shepherd be, and near
Still remain thy rock and shield,
  When thy heart's oppress'd with fear.
When of need thou feel'st the smart,
  May He press thee to His heart.
Dost thou sit or rise again,
  Dost thou speak or dost thou hear,
Still at home dost thou remain,
  Art abroad when none is near,
Dost thou wander in or out?
  He will compass thee about.

THE 139TH PSALM OF DAVID.

Lord, Thou my heart dost search and try,
  And what is hidden from mine eye
Thou seest, all I am and own
To Thine omniscient mind is known.
Whene'r I sit, lie down, or stand,
  Or walk, or run, on ev'ry hand
Thy presence doth encompass me,
  At all times I am hard by Thee.
And all the thoughts that stir my heart,
  That lurk in its most secret part,
Thy searching eye doth scrutinize
Ere they to consciousness arise.
And never from my tongue a word
  Escapes, by Thee, O Lord, unheard;
Thou order'st all I speak or do,
  And guidest me life's journey through.
[139]
'Tis true, I know, but must remain
  A knowledge I can ne'er attain,
  A mystery beyond the ken
Of feeble and short-sighted men.
Where shall I from Thy Spirit fly,
  Escape from Thine omniscient eye?
  Where shall I from Thy presence hide,
  And where remote from Thee abide?
If I ascend the utmost height
  Of heav'n, there art Thou, thron'd in light;

Or should I down to hell repair
  And make my bed, I'd find Thee there.
Should I on morning's pinions ride,
  As far as ocean's empire wide
  Of stormy waves breaks on the land,
  I'd be upheld by Thy right hand.
Or if the help of night I sought,
  No change by darkness would be wrought,
  For let the night be as it may,
  With Thee is ever cloudless day.
[140]
'Mid darkest shadows Thou canst see,
  The darkness is a light to Thee,
  Thy glance is ever clear and bright,
From sun and moon Thou need'st no light.
My reins Thou ever hast possess'd,
  For in Thy hand they ever rest,
  From infancy Thou hast me led,
  With daily blessings crown'd my head.
Thou hast, who'rt greatly to be fear'd,
  My frame with cunning hand uprear'd;
  Thy works, Thy wondrous pow'r forth tell,
  And that my soul doth know right well.
My substance was not hid from Thee,
  When I in secret curiously
  Was fashion'd in the depths of earth,
  From whence Thy pow'r hath brought me forth.
Before my time, my times for me
  Determin'd were by Thy decree,
  The tale of years and days I'd see,
  Hours, moments, all were fix'd by Thee.
[141]
My God, how precious, sweet, and fair,
  I see array'd before me there
  The thoughts of wisdom of Thy heart,
  In all Thy bounty doth impart.
The sum of these so high doth mount,
  That when their number I would count,
  I find them infinitely more
  Than dust or sand, on field or shore.
How doth the bold blaspheming band
  Thee vilify on every hand,
  O God of wonders! and Thy name
  Despise and treat with open shame.
Their scornful mouths, Lord, close and seal,
  Against them speedily reveal
  Thy wrath! against Thy foes arise,
  Thy foes are hateful in mine eyes.
Though in return, their hatred sore
  Against Thee burn, I do no more
  Amid the rage of angry foes,
  Than 'neath Thy shelt'ring wings repose.
[142]
Lord, search and know my heart and mood,
  See if my way be right and good,
  The everlasting joyful road
  Lead me that brings me home to God.
[143]

Songs of the Cross and Consolation.

UNDER THE TRIALS OF THIS LIFE.

Full often as I meditate
  Upon the world's disorder'd state,
  I ask myself if earthly life
  Be good, and worthy of the strife,
  Has he not acted for the best
  Who laid himself betimes to rest?
Reflect, my friend, say, if you know
  What station is there here below
  Without its fall and daily share
  Of sorrow, pain, and anxious care?
  And tell me if a place there be
  From sorrow, tears, vexation free.
And doth not every passing day,
  From youth to manhood, bear away
[144]
Its own peculiar load of grief
  Upon its back, and such relief
  As transient joy may seem to bring,
  Is it not full of suffering?
If times be good, and fortune smile,
  My God! how envy storms the while;
  If dignity and honours great
  Attend thy steps, alas! their weight.
  If others thou'rt preferr'd before,
  Than others too thou'rt burden'd more.
Art thou to-day in joyous mood,
  Rejoicing in thy share of good?
  Lo! ere thou think'st, thy gains are gone,
  Thy joyous mood with them is flown,
  The hurricane so suddenly
  Doth sweep away thy property.
Dost from the world withdraw thyself,
  And lov'st God more than gold or

pelf?
  Thy crown, thy jewel, thy good name
  Is cover'd by the world with shame.
  For he who can't dissembler play,
  The world as fool will spurn away.
[145]
'Tis true, alas! that trouble waits
  In daily watch before our gates;
  On earth the cross is borne by all,
  All feel its weight, and taste its gall;
  But shall we therefore cast away
  The Christian's light? I tell thee—nay.
The saints, who to their Saviour cleave,
  In faith and in the Spirit live,
  Unhurt by any ill or woe
  Pass through their pilgrimage below;
  Though things may sometimes fall out ill
  Yet with them it is ever well.
Though they no gold have stor'd away,
  They've God, and care not what men say,
  Reject with joy, and aye despise
  The world's vain pomp and vanities;
  Their honour is to hope and wait,
  From God alone comes all their state.
The Christian, God as Father knows,
  Can in His faithfulness repose;
[146]
Whatever trial God may send,
  Can't separate him from his friend;
  The more He smites, he loves the more,
  Remaineth true, though chasten'd sore.
He only plays a hero's part
  Who cherishes within his heart
  The Saviour's love; whate'er betide,
  Firm as a rock shall he abide
  When heav'n and earth shall pass away;
  Though men forsake, God's word's his stay.
The word of God beguiles our fears,
  And turns to smiles our bitter tears;
  It robs misfortune of the pow'r
  Of hurting in the evil hour;
  It brings the sadden'd heart relief,
  When bow'd beneath the load of grief.
Now cease, I pray, your tale of woe:
  Though full of grief this life below,
  Still falleth to the Christian's share
  Salvation and God's guardian care;
  Who loves the Saviour, trusts in God,
  Remains unmov'd beneath the rod.
[147]
As gold into the fire is cast,
  And comes forth purified at last,
  So saints supported by God's grace
  Uninjur'd through affliction pass;
  A child his father's child is still,
  Although his father's rod he feel.
Dear heart, chase all thy fears away,
  On thy God's faithfulness now stay,
  Though smiting with His chast'ning rod,
  He means it well, 'tis for thy good;
  Confide in Him, His guiding hand
  Will bring thee to the better land.
Live on according to His will,
  Although the way be rough, be still!
  In heav'n Thou hast a mansion fair,
  Where joy will banish every care;
  If here we to the Saviour cleave,
  With Jesu's angels shall we live.
[148]

THOU ART BUT MAN!

Thou art but man, to thee 'tis known,
  Why dost thou then endeavour
  To do what God should do alone,
  Or can accomplish ever?
  A thousand griefs thou goest through,
  In spite of all thy wit can do;
  Upon thine end thou pond'rest,
  What it will be thou wond'rest.
'Tis all in vain, in vain thy care,
  With all thy musings earnest,
  In all thy life a single hair
  Thou white or black ne'er turnest.
  The griefs by which thou'rt sore distress'd
  Can only serve to mar thy rest,
  Cause anguish unavailing,
  Thy life itself curtailing.
Wilt thou do what is for thy good,
  And what thy God good seeth?
  Then cast on Him each heavy load,
  'Fore whom earth and heav'n fleeth.
[149]
Thy life and labour, all that's thine,
  With joy into God's hand resign;
  A happy end He'll ever
  Give thee, and thee deliver.
Who car'd for thee ere light of day
  Had dawn'd upon thy vision,
  While in the womb thy soul still lay
  As in a gloomy prison?
  Who thought upon thy welfare then?
  What good did all the might of men
  Do, when to thee were given
  Life, mind, and pow'r from heaven?
Whose skill was it that fashion'd thee?
  And who thy frame uprearèd?
  To glad our eyes, by whose decree,
  Say, hath the light appearèd?
  Who hath thy veins in order laid,
  For each a course convenient made?
  Who hath thy frame replenish'd
  With members fair and finish'd?
[150]
Where were thy mind and will and heart
  When land and ocean over,
  Yea, even earth's remotest part,
  The sky was spread to cover?
  Who made the sun and moon to shine,
  Who gave herbs, trees, and beasts as thine,
  Who bid them satisfy thee,
  And no desire deny thee?
Lift up thy head, see everywhere,
  Above, around, below thee,
  How God in all for thee His care,
  And at all times, doth show thee!
  Thy meat and drink, the clothes dost wear,
  Did God, ere need thou felt'st, prepare.
  God, ere thou wast, prepar'd thee
  Thy mother's milk, that rear'd thee.
The raiment that in infancy
  Thy nakedness did cover,
  The cradle that receivèd thee,
  The roof thy young head over,
[151]
Were all in love prepar'd for thee,
  Ere yet thine eye was op'd to see
  The wonders that abounded,
  The world that thee surrounded.
Yet wilt thou walk by thine own light
  Thy life long, only heeding,
  Believing nothing but thy sight,
  Go whither it is leading.
  In all that thou dost undertake,
  Thy heart thy counsellor dost make,
  Unless by it selected,
  Is ev'ry plan rejected.
Behold! how oft and openly
  God's providence undoeth
  The plans thy hand so ardently
  And hopefully pursueth.
  But it doth happen frequently,
  That e'en the very things we see

The wisest men could never
   Predict, or think of ever.
[152]
How oft thy stiff-neck'd self-will hath
   To bitter need reduc'd thee!
When heart and mind deluded, death
   To take for life, seduc'd thee!
And had the Lord thy work and deed
   Along the path allow'd proceed
That thou thyself had'st taken,
   Lost wert thou and forsaken.
He who to us love endless feels,
   When self-involv'd, then frees us,
Ev'n self-inflicted wounds He heals,
   Guides when astray He sees us.
Paternal kindness, tender love,
   To these His heart doth ever move,
This love poor sinners beareth,
   For whom as sons He careth.
Ah! silence doth He often keep,
   But still the while He blesses,
E'en though we tears of anguish weep,
   Though grief the heart depresses,
[153]
Although our eager eyes we strain,
   And seek for light, but seek in vain,
And seek deliv'rance ever
   From woe, but find it never.
But God our Lord still onward straight
   His path pursueth ever,
And brings us to heav'n's peaceful gate,
   Where storms assail us never.
What dark was and mysterious here
In all God's ways, shall be then clear,
   His wisdom we'll discover
   When our life-work is over.
Then peace, be still, my troubled breast!
   And let no grief distress thee,
God ever plans for thee the best,
   His heart is set to bless thee.
Thy cause the Saviour ne'er can leave,
   In this assuredly believe,
Tow'rd us He ever yearneth,
   His ardent love aye burneth.
[154]
With grace and truth His loving heart
   For evermore is glowing,
And keenly feeleth He the smart,
   When from our eyes are flowing
Hot tears, caus'd by vain sorrow's load,
   As if in wrath and hate our God

Could ever helpless leave us,
   Would never comfort give us!
The evil thought, ah! put away,
   No more may it deceive thee,
Although what happ'neth, seldom may
   Increase of pleasure give thee.
But that will happen certainly
   Which God thy Father doth decree;
From what He wills to send thee,
   No mortal can defend thee.
Then to thy Father's arms of love
   In confidence betake thee,
Pray on till His compassion move,
   His special care He make thee!
[155]
Then by His Spirit will He guide,
   Through unknown paths still at thy side,
   From all thy woe and striving
   At last deliv'rance giving.

CHRISTIAN CONTENTMENT.
O my soul, why dost thou grieve,
   Why dost mourn so bitterly,
That more freely God doth give
   Gifts to others than to thee?
In thy God delight thy heart,
He's the good enduring part.
Of the human race have none
   In this world to be a right,
All, yea each created one,
   But a guest is for a night.
God in His house Lord is still,
Gifts divideth as He will.
[156]
Know, thou art not therefore here,
   That thou should'st possess the earth;
Look thou up to heav'n so clear,
   There's thy gold of priceless worth,
There is honour, there is joy,
Without envy or alloy!
Great the folly his who grieves
   For a little vanity,
When God to him freely gives
   Treasures of eternity.
Is the handredweight thy gain?
Thou canst then despise the grain.
All thy fair possessions see,
   That are valued by thy heart,
None of them can go with thee
   When from earth thou must depart.
Thou must leave them here below,
When death's door thou passest through.
The soul's nourishment, God's grace,

And the Saviour's precious blood,
   Ne'er through time in worth decrease,
   But remain for ever good.
[157]
Earthly goods must pass away,
   Soul-goods never can decay.
Still art thou so blind, alas!
   Thinking—but all erringly,
Eyes hast thou, but in the glass
   Of the word thou dost not see.
Child of man! fix there thine eyes,
For it is a peerless prize.
Count thy fingers every one,
   And thine other members o'er,
They are precious, they're thine own,
   Lov'd by thee than treasure more,
Gold could never from thee buy
E'en the least, though men should try.
Search and ask thine inmost heart,
   'Twill instruct thee what of good
Daily falleth to thy part,
   By God's bounteous hand bestow'd;
Than the sand upon the shore
More, and yet desir'st thou more!
[158]
Did thy Heav'nly Father see
   That it would be for thy good,
What desires so eagerly
   Thy misguided flesh and blood,
He would ne'er thee joyless leave,
But would of His bounty give.
God to thee is full of love,
   Faithful and sincere is He,
When thou wishest aught, He'd prove
   Of what kind thy wish may be:
If 'tis good, He will bestow,
If 'tis ill, He'll answer—no.
Meanwhile doth His Spirit give
   Manna to thy fainting heart,
Food by which the angels live,
   Grace to deck thee doth impart,
For His portion chooseth thee,
Thou shalt share salvation free.
Look then to thy God above,
   Sad and troubled countenance!
Cease to sigh, faith's virtue prove,
   By thy clear and joyous glance!
[159]
While thy sky is overcast
   By affliction, hold it fast!
And as Heav'n's adopted son,
   Thy rebellious will restrain;
Touch thy harp, let 'fore God's throne

Grateful songs resound again.
More at all times doth God give
Than thou'rt worthy to receive.
Live thou ever in God's fear,
   As thou journeyest to heav'n,
   Take whate'er befalls thee here
   As a gift in wisdom giv'n.
   Are they evil days, thou'lt see
God and Heav'n endure for thee.
[160]

UNDER THE VEXATIONS OF THE WICKED PROSPEROUS WORLD.

Ah! lovely innocence, how evil art thou deem'd,
   How lightly oft thy work by all the world's esteem'd!
   Thou servest God, thy Lord, and to His word thou cleavest;
   For this, from men thou nought but scorn and hate receivest.
Right on thy road thou go'st, flee'st from the crooked way;
   Another steppeth in and bears the prize away,
   Increaseth his small store, his chests and barns he filleth;
   Thou'rt poor with all thy house, scarce earn'st what hunger stilleth.
The wicked one thou chid'st, who walks not righteously,
   Another practiseth a sweet hypocrisy
[161]
That love and praise secures, and him on high upraises,
   While in the lurch the world thee leaves, and much abases.
Thou say'st that virtue is the Christian's fairest crown,
   But reputation doth the world lay stress upon;
   He who will this secure, it saith, must ever labour
   To suit the times, and live and act just like his neighbour.
Thou boast'st thyself in God, thy tongue doth aye commend
   The blessing God doth as His children's portion send:
   "If this be then the case," the world says, "come and show it,
   The happy fortune thou hast had, we'd see and know it."
Stand firm, thou pious heart, stand firm, thy faith retain!
   'Mid disappointment sore thy God will true remain,
   Commit thy ways to Him, let Him protect and guide thee,
   Thou'lt triumph at the last o'er evils that betide thee.
[162]
Dost fail to please thy kind?—It is a sad disgrace!
   Enough, if on thee smile thy heav'nly Father's face.
   The worst that man can do is to betray and leave thee;
   But God is righteous, and His judgment can't deceive thee.
Doth He say, "Thou art Mine, thy way doth please Me well?"
   Then be thy heart consol'd, let joy thy bosom swell,
   Cast to the wind the lies by wicked men indited,
   Be still, and thou shalt see, by God shall all be righted.
Pride, arrogance, and pomp are ne'er enduring found,
   Like brightest glass they fall, and break upon the ground;
   So when the luck of men has mounted up to heaven,
   It soon comes crashing down, and on the earth lies riven.
And all ill-gotten wealth, when right our estimate,
   Is on the heart and mind a dead oppressive weight
[163]
That burdens evermore, with pain the conscience wringeth,
   Its quiet rest disturbs, and into trouble bringeth.
And what have many more than of the poor the sweat?
   What do they eat and drink, and what gain do they get?
   They rob the widows' store, spite of their tears them wronging,
   Who like a thirsty land for sympathy are longing.
Is this felicity? is this magnificence?
   Oh! what a sentence dire will God the Judge pronounce
   Upon the day of doom, when from His throne so loudly
   It sounds, how shall they seem who strut and boast so proudly!
But thou who now thy God dost honour with whole heart,
   And never from His ways dost let thy feet depart,
   Shalt in the goodly throng, whom God with manna feedeth,
   With praise and honour clad, walk with Him where he leadeth.
[164]
In patience, then, possess thy soul a little while,
   Do right, and persevere and live all free from guile,
   Act that the fairest prize in yonder life be given
   Thee, from His gracious hand who rules in earth and heaven.
Whate'er on earth betide, from care remain all free,
   'Twill fall out for thy good, as God the best may see;
   Rest thou assur'd, He will no wish of thine deny thee,
   With joy fulfil thy will, with every good supply thee.
[165]

"I WILL ENDURE THE INDIGNATION OF THE LORD."—MICAH VII.

I have deserv'd it, cease t' oppose
   The Lord's will, shall I never?
   Thou bitter cup, thou heavy cross,
   Come hither to me ever!
   From pain all free
   May never be
He 'gainst the Lord who fighteth,
   As I each day,
   Who trod the way
Wherein the world delighteth.
I'll bear the chastisement of God,
   A patient soul possessing,
For born in sin, sin's path I trod,
   Aye ventur'd on transgressing,
   That pleasures vain
   I might attain,
In wantonness time wasting,
   The gracious word
   Of God the Lord,
   As I ought, never tasting.
[166]
The road of God's commandments good
   I often have forsaken,
And on the way that leads from God
Am therefore overtaken

By grief and smart,
That pierce my heart;
God's hand thus am I feeling,
Who 'fore His throne
To each his own
Awards, in justice dealing.
For just and true is God above,
We fail His goodness telling,
A mother's truth, a father's love
Alike in him are dwelling.
God's wrath, I ween,
As oft hath been
Ours, is not unrelenting.
Men steel their heart,
Refuse t' impart
Grace e'en to the repenting.

[167]
In sooth 'tis not the mind of God,
His anger ever endeth,
Return we, He removes the rod,
And to the weary sendeth
A sweet release,
To mark doth cease,
And visit our transgressing;
His wrath He turns,
And tow'rd us yearns,
Gives after cursing blessing.
And so the Lord will deal with me,
And every one behold it,
And vindicate the right will He,
My cause, He will uphold it.
Thy face so bright,
Lord! to the light,
From deepest pit will raise me,
That ever I
May heartily
Thy truth exalt, and praise Thee.

[168]
Rejoice not o'er me, then, my foes,
I lie not here for ever,
My God will come ere ye suppose,
And speedily deliver.
His holy hand
Will make me stand,
Firm and secure for ever;
Good times to me
And joy will He
Give after stormy weather.
I am in need, yet scarce can speak
Of real need and sorrow;
When God my Light is, day must break
And bring a glorious morrow,
E'en in the night,
While yet the might
Of darkness much increaseth,
And when this Light
Dawns on my sight,
Whate'er oppresses ceaseth.

[169]
The time will come, e'en now 'tis near,
When I shall sing salvation,
When he who lov'd to mock and jeer
At me in tribulation,
And bid me tell
Where God doth dwell,
Shall from God's face be driven
With head cast down;
To me a crown
Of honour shall be given!

FOR PATIENCE IN GREAT SORROW.

Ah! faithful God, compass'nate heart,
Whose goodness never endeth,
I know this bitter cross and smart
Thy hand it is that sendeth!
Yea, Lord, I know this burden great
Thou sendest not in wrath and hate,
But 'tis in love appointed.

[170]
That ever is Thy way all-wise,
Thy child in woe must languish,
Thou whom Thou lovest, dost chastise,
'Fore joy Thou sendest anguish,
Sink'st us to hell, in woe we lie,
And raisest us again on high,
Thus with us fares it always.
Thou ever leadest wondrously
Thy children dear who please Thee!
Would I have life? Then first must I
E'en down to death abase me.
In honour who'd be raised on high,
He self-abas'd on earth must lie
As worthless dust and ashes.
On earth, Lord, Thy belovèd Son
Such sorrow had to try Him;
Ere He could reach His glorious throne
Ill men must crucify Him.
He pass'd through trouble, need, and woe,
Nor shrunk He from death's cruel blow,
To reach the joys of heaven.

[171]
Did then Thy good and holy Son
Himself for us deliver,
And I enslavèd, sinful one,
Shall I resist Thee ever?
Of patience aye the glass is He,
And who His face desires to see
Must in His footsteps follow.
How is it reason finds it hard,
The truth so oft rejecteth,
That Thou with favour dost regard
E'en while Thy hand afflicteth?
How long doth oft the cross remain,
How hardly can we love and pain
Then reconcile together.
God of the Church! when fails my pow'r,
Strength graciously then give me;
And grant that nought in trial's hour
Of faith may e'er deprive me.
Uphold me by Thy might, O Lord,
Establish me then in Thy word,
From murmuring deliver!

[172]
When I am weak, be Thou my stay,
In faithfulness be near me,
That I continually may pray,
And call on Thee to hear me.
While yet a heart hopes and believes,
And still in pray'r unceasing lives,
Bold is it, and unvanquish'd.
In measure, Lord, apply the rod,
Lest I sink altogether;
Thou know'st how I can bear the load,
How life's imperill'd ever,
For neither steel nor stone am I,
But sooner pass away and die,
E'en than a fleeting vapour.
Ah! Jesus, who did'st stoop so low,
Thy blood shed, life that giveth,
The bitter cross full well dost know,
And how the spirit grieveth
When cross and heavy woe combine,
So wilt Thou hear each cry of mine,
When bitterly complaining.

[173]
I know Thou feelest sympathy
When want and woe distress me,
That Thou with help wilt visit me,
And graciously wilt bless me.
Ah! strengthen Thou my feeble hand,
And lead my feet where I may stand
In safety—Come and save me!
Speak courage to my fainting heart,
With comfort, Lord, support me.
Of weary souls the Rest Thou art,
My Tow'r, where none can hurt me!
My Rock, where from the sun I hide,
My Tent, where safely I abide

When storms without are raging!
And as in love, while here I dwell,
   Thou suff'ring hast decreed me,
Thy grace vouchsafe Thy child, Lord, still,
   In Thy green pastures lead me;
That I in faith may patience gain,
Through patience rich reward attain,
   When I've endur'd the trial.

[174]

Oh! Holy Ghost, of joy the Oil,
   Whom God from Heaven giveth,
Refresh me, pour into my soul
   What heart and flesh reviveth.
Of glory, Thou the Spirit art,
Know'st what in heav'n shall be my part
   Of grace, joy, consolation!
How fair 'twill be, ah! let me gaze
   Upon the life so glorious,
That Thou wilt give to those who pass
   Through trials sore, victorious.
The earth with all its treasures fair
Can never with this life compare,
   They pale and fade before it.
Thou'lt deal with me so graciously,
   I'll endless joy be tasting,
For trials known to Thee and me
   Have glory everlasting.
Thou'lt wipe the tear-drop from mine eyes,
   To exultation turn my sighs,
   Lord! I believe it. Amen!

[175]

UNDER THE CROSS WHEN GOD DELAYS HIS HELP.

Father of mercies! God most high,
   Deign graciously to hear me,
Thou say'st, "Knock at my door and cry,
   In time of need draw near me.
   As urgently
   Thou long'st, to thee
I'll come to help and raise thee,
   That with thy mouth,
   In very truth,
Thou joyfully may'st praise me."
Commit to God, both morn and night,
   Thy ways, and doings ever;
He knoweth how to guide thee right,
   And always will deliver.
   To Him reveal
   Whate'er dost feel
Thy heart to sorrow moveth;
   He is Thy Lord,
   Knows how to guard
And shield thee whom He loveth.

[176]

For His belovèd child will care
   The faithful loving Father;
Who righteous and believing are,
   He to His rest will gather.
   Then, people dear,
   Hope ever here
On Him who aye relieves you;
   His throne before
   Your hearts outpour,
Tell Him whatever grieves you!
Ah! God our Shield! Thy word how sweet
   It sounds to Thine afflicted:
"I'll come to thee with succour meet,
   When thy heart is dejected.
   He loveth me,
   So lov'd shall be,
Secure for aye I'll make him,
   From care all free
   Shall sit by me,
I'll to my bosom take him."

[177]

The Lord to them is ever nigh
   Who trustfully draw near Him,
He's at their side whene'er they cry,
   Helps them o'ercome, who fear Him.
   In misery
   Who low do lie,
He raiseth and relieveth,
   And joy imparts
   To fainting hearts,
Them pow'r and might he giveth.
"In truth, who my great name doth fear,"
   Saith Christ, "and firm believeth,
God doth regard his pray'r sincere,
   His heart's wish freely giveth."
   Then one and all
   Draw near and call,
Who asketh, he obtaineth;
   Who seeketh there,
   The fruit so fair
With great advantage gaineth.

[178]

Hear what yon unjust judge doth say:
   "This widow's supplication
I must regard, lest day by day
   Her coming cause vexation."
   His people's cry
   Shall God deny,
Who day and night are praying?
   It cannot be,
   He'll set them free
From woe, not long delaying.
For when the just shed tears through care,
   God soon with joy relieveth,
To those who broken-hearted are,
   Again He laughter giveth.
   He'll suffer woe
   Who will below
'Mid men be godly living;
   But at his side
   Will God abide,
Him grace sufficient giving.

[179]

"A moment I've forsaken thee,
   And left thee in temptation;
With mercy great, as thou shalt see,
   And boundless consolation,
   I'll give the crown,
   And to the throne
Of glory shall I raise thee,
   To joy convert
   Thy grief and hurt,
Thou evermore shalt praise me."
Ah! gracious God, ah! Father's heart!
   For years my consolation!
Why dost Thou let me feel such smart,
   Pass through such tribulation?
   My sad heart aches,
   My eye awakes,
And bitter tears sheds ever,
   My face once bright
   Doth lose its light,
From sighing ceasing never.

[180]

How long, O blessèd Lord! wilt Thou,
   Unmindful of me, leave me?
How long shall I in grief lie low,
   And inward sorrow grieve me?
   How long wilt chide,
   And Thy face hide,
In darkness let me languish?
   Say, when care's load
   Shall cease, my God!
To wring my heart with anguish?
Wilt Thou eternally repel,
   And show Thy goodness never?
And shall Thy word and promise fail,
   Be put to shame for ever?
   Doth wrath so burn,
   That Thou'lt ne'er turn
To me, and stand beside me?
   Yet, Lord, I will

Cleave to Thee still,
Thy hand in all can guide me.
[181]
My heart amid earth's misery
   For Thee, O Lord! is aching;
My God! I wait and hope in Thee,
   Let not shame me o'ertaking;
Thy friend in woe
Plunge, or the foe
Give cause for jubilation;
   But, Lord, may I
   Rejoice, rais'd high,
In glorious exaltation.
Ah! Lord, Thou true and faithful art,
   Thy heart can ne'er disown me;
Nerve me in fight to bear my part,
   With victory then crown me!
Lay Thou on me
The load, by Thee
Appointed, that I bear it.
   When Thou the rod
   Dost use, my God!
In measure may I share it!
[182]
Thy strength, O Lord! is infinite,
   Thy hand hath all created,
Could all again with ruin smite,
   Its pow'r is unabated.
We sound Thy name
With high acclaim,
As Lord of Hosts we own Thee!
   In counsel right
   No skill nor might
Can foil, nor e'er dethrone Thee.
Thou who dost Israel console,
   Thou, Saviour, in affliction!
Ah! why permittest Thou my soul
   To sink in sore dejection?
Thou dost not rest,
Thou'rt as a guest,
Who'rt in the land a stranger!
   A hero Thou
   Whose courage low
Sinks 'fore disgrace or danger?
[183]
Nay, Lord, not such a one art Thou!
   My inmost heart believeth;
Thou standest firm, 'mid us shines now
   The light that Thy word giveth.
Here restest Thou,
Lord, with us now;
Who call upon Thee ever,
   At fitting hour
   Wilt by Thy pow'r
From ev'ry woe deliver.
O Lord! my lengthen'd tale is o'er,
   Then hear Thou my petition,
Help me, who often at Thy door
   Have knock'd, and sought admission.
Help, Helper, me!
I'll joyfully
Thankoff'rings lay before Thee;
   And when life's o'er
   Shall evermore
In heav'n above adore Thee.
[184]

'TIS PATIENCE MUST SUPPORT YOU.—HEB. X. 35-37.

'Tis patience must support you
   When sorrow, grief, or smart,
Or whate'er else may hurt you,
   Doth rend your aching heart.
Belov'd and chosen seed!
If not a death will kill you,
Yet once again I tell you,
   'Tis patience that you need.
The cup of patience drinketh
   With nausea flesh and blood,
Back from the cross it shrinketh;
   When threaten'd with the rod,
It shuddereth with fear.
'Tis bold when nought assaileth,
Heart shrinks, and courage faileth,
   When storms and rain are here.
Why patience causeth sadness,
   Is that the carnal mind
Unclouded joy and gladness
   In God aye hop'd to find,
[185]
Though He hath made it clear,
   He chastens whom He loveth,
And whom He much approveth,
   He much afflicteth here.
God giveth patience ever,
   The Spirit in the breast
Begetteth it whenever
   Within us He doth rest;
The worthy, noble Guest
Preserves us from despairing,
And nerves for burden-bearing
   The heart when sore distress'd.
From faith all patience springeth,
   On God's own word depends,
To this she firmly clingeth,
   Herself with this defends.
'Tis her high tow'r and wall,
Where she securely hideth,
Where God for her provideth,
   Here fears she ne'er a fall.
[186]
And patience trust reposeth
   On Jesu's death and pain;
When Satan her opposeth,
   Here takes she heart again,
And saith, "Thou Prince of hell!
Thou never shalt devour me,
Too high I'm lifted o'er thee,
   In Jesus do I dwell."
Contented patience stayeth
   On God's decree all-wise;
Although His grace delayeth,
   Scarce feels fatigue arise;
With trust she bears her load,
And joyfully endureth,
This thought her heart assureth,
   It is the hand of God.
Long, long, can patience waiting
   The weary time beguile,
On God's word meditating
   Get saving good the while.
[187]
With earnest fervent pray'r,
Each morn and eve she guardeth
Herself from ill, and wardeth
   Off Satan's every snare.
To God's will patience boweth,
   Doth His command fulfil,
'Mid scorn of foes she knoweth
   'Tis wisest to be still.
Who will, let him despise,
Unhurt by the dishonour
And shame thus put upon her,
   Her heart doth o'er it rise.
To honour patience serveth
   Her God, and never more
From love and fealty swerveth;
   Although He smiteth sore,
Yet doth she ever praise
His holy hand, and telleth
That God on high who dwelleth,
   Doth well in all his ways.
[188]
And patience life sustaineth,
   Adds to our tale of years;
She drives away what paineth
   The heart, and stills its fears.
It is a beauteous light
That giveth him who heedeth,
And whom God's guidance leadeth,
   A face with joy all bright.
Great joy from patience springeth,
   The head a noble crown,
Gems for the neck she bringeth
   From throne of Heaven down.

She wipes from weeping eyes
The tears of grief and anguish;
Whose souls with longing languish,
With ample good supplies.
My soul for patience sigheth,
My heart longs eagerly,
How urgently it crieth
And oft is known to Thee,

[189]
Of grace who hast full store!
Lord, hear my supplication,
Give patient resignation;
I ask for nothing more.
For patience the petition
Shall often up to Thee,
From out my low condition,
Ascend, O Lord, from me.
And in my dying hour,
Thy mercy still extending,
Oh! grant a patient ending,
Then need I nothing more.

WHAT PLEASETH GOD!

What pleaseth God, my faithful child,
Receive with joy; although the wild
And wintry wind thy heart appal,
Have faith, thee only can befal
What pleaseth God!

[190]
The will of God is aye the best,
In it we can so calmly rest;
Thyself to it anew resign,
And only seek to have as thine
What pleaseth God!
God's counsel is the only wise;
Soon comes to nought what men devise;
Their projects fall, fall out of use,
Oft mischief work, not oft produce
What pleaseth God!
God's mood is the most gracious mood,
To all intending, doing good;
He blesses, though hard words may speak
The wicked world, and never seek
What pleaseth God!
The truest heart is God's own heart,
Who bids our misery depart;
Who screens and shelters, day and night,
The man who makes his chief delight
What pleaseth God!

[191]
Ah! could I sing, as sing I would,
From out my heart, and ever should,
I'd ope my mouth—in Him rejoice,
This moment praise with heart and voice
What pleaseth God!
His counsel wise would I make known,
The works of wonder He hath done;
His saving grace, eternal pow'r,
That work producing every hour
What pleaseth God.
He rules above and rules below;
On Him hangs all our weal and woe;
He bears the world in His high hand,
For us brings forth the sea and land
What pleaseth God!
His hands the elements restrain;
His hands our mortal life sustain—
Give summer, winter, day, and night,
That evermore to do delight
What pleaseth God!

[192]
His host, the stars, the moon, and sun,
Their wonted courses ever run;
Corn, oil, and must, bread, wine, and beer,
The fruitful earth brings forth each year,
Which pleaseth God!
His understanding is all wise,
He knows—they are before his eyes,
Who evil think and evil do,
As well as who the good pursue
That pleaseth God!
His little flock to Him is dear;
When sinning they forsake His fear,
He chastens with His Father's rod,
Till they return and do the good
That pleaseth God!
What cheers and strengtheneth our heart
He knows, and ever doth impart
Whatever good each one requires,
Who seeks for good and aye desires
What pleaseth God!

[193]
Is't so? then let the world retain
What pleaseth her, and she deems gain;
But thou in God delighted be,
My heart! approve whate'er you see
That pleaseth God!
Let others then in haughty mood
Rejoice in stores of earthly good;
But thou the Cross with patience bear,
Contented if thou hast the share
That pleaseth God!
Dost live in sorrow, sunk in grief,
Hast much affliction—no relief?
Still murmur not, for thou dost bear
In this thy bitter life of care
What pleaseth God!
In suff'rings art thou doom'd to live?
Then to thy great Protector cleave;
The world and all the creatures too
Are under God, can only do
What pleaseth God!

[194]
Doth ev'ry one despise Thy name?
Do foes Thee scorn and treat with shame?
Be not cast down, for Christ will raise
Thy head, who seeth in thy ways
What pleaseth God!
Faith fastens on the Saviour's love
Works patience, hope that looks above;
Lock both within thy secret heart,
Thou'lt have as thine eternal part
What pleaseth God!
Thy part is in the Heav'nly throne,
There is thy sceptre, kingdom, crown;
There shalt thou taste, and hear, and see,
There shall for ever happen thee
What pleaseth God!

[195]

IN DESPONDENCY AND TEMPTATION.

Look up to thy God again,
Soul, sunk in affliction!
Shall He be reproach'd by men
Through thy sore dejection?
Satan's wiles dost thou not see?
By severe temptation,
Gladly would he keep from thee
Jesu's consolation.
Shake thy head in scorn, and "flee,"
Bid the old deceiver—
"Wilt renew thy thrusts at me,
Me to fear deliver?
Serpent! bruis'd thy head I see;
Through His pain hath freed me
From thy grasp, my Lord, and He
To His joy will lead me.
"Dost thou charge my sin to me?
When did God command me
Judgment to require from thee?
Tell me, I demand thee!

[196]
Who did pow'r on thee bestow
Sentence to deliver?

Who thyself art sunk so low
   In hell's flames for ever."
What I have not done aright
   Me with sorrow filleth,
But of Jesu's blood the sight
   All mine anguish stilleth.
He the ransom price hath paid,
   From the cross relieves me,
When before God's throne 'tis laid,
   Inward joy He gives me.
In Christ's innocence I boast,
   His right is my glory,
Mine His merit, there I trust
   As in stronghold hoary,
That the rage of every foe
   Evermore resisteth,
Though the might of hell below
   It to storm assisteth.
[197]
Rage then, devil, and thou, death!
   Ye can never hurt me;
In the trials of my path
   Doth God's grace support me.
God His only Son to me,
   Mov'd by love, hath given,
That to endless misery
   I may not be driven.
Cry then, foolish world! amain,
   That God lov'd me never,
That my cherish'd hope is vain,
   Has deceiv'd me ever.
Had God been averse to me,
   Would He have supported
All the gifts so rich and free
   He to me imparted?
What is there in sky or sea,
   What the wide earth over,
What that works no good for me,
   Canst thou then discover?
[198]
Why do star so beauteously
   Shine on us from Heaven?
Why are, but for good to me,
   Air and water given?
Why do clouds their streams outpour?
   Why do dews earth cover?
Why with verdure's cover'd o'er,
   Why flow blessings over
Hill and valley, field and wood?
   Truly for my pleasure,
That I dwell secure, and food
   Have in plenteous measure.
My soul on God's word most dear
   Feeds and liveth ever,
That all Christians love to hear
   Daily, tiring never.
Soon and late my heart in me
   God opes for receiving
Of the Spirit's grace that He
   Is so freely giving.
[199]
Why through holy men of old
   Have God's words been given?
That we by their light might hold
   On our way to heaven,
My heart's darkness to dispel,
   From doubt to deliver,
That the conscience sure and well,
   Be establish'd ever.
Now upon this holy ground
   Build I most securely,
See how hell's malicious hound,
   Spends 'gainst me his fury.
He can never overthrow
   What God hath upraisèd,
But what Satan's hand doth do
   That shall be abasèd.
I am God's, and mine is God,
   Who from Him can part me?
Tho' the cross with heavy load
   Press on me and smart me.
[200]
Let it press—the hand of love
   Hath the cross laid on me,
He the burden will remove,
   When the good is done me.
Children whom aright to guide
   Parents would endeavour,
Must the father often chide,
   Or they'd prosper never.
If I'm then a child of grace,
   Should I shun God ever,
When He from sin's devious ways,
   Seeks me to deliver?
Gracious are the thoughts of God,
   In the pain He's sending,
Who here weeps beneath the rod,
   Reaps not woe unending,
But eternal joy shall taste
   In Christ's garden dwelling,
That he shall be there at last,
   Now assurance feeling.
[201]
Often God's own children here
   Sow in tears and sadness,
But at length the long'd-for year
   Comes of joy and gladness;
For the reaping time appears,
   All their labours after,
When are turn'd their grief and tears
   Into joy and laughter.
Christian heart! courageously
   All the griefs that pain thee
Cast behind thee joyfully,
   More and more sustain thee
Let sweet consolation's light;
   Praise and honour give you
To the God of love and might,
   He'll help and relieve you.
[202]

BE THOU CONTENTED.

Be thou contented! aye relying
   On thy God, who life is giving,
For He hath joys soul satisfying,
   Wanting Him—in vain thy striving.
   Thy Spring is He,
   Thy Sun that ever
   Rejoiceth thee,
   And setteth never.
   Be thou contented!
He lightens, comforts, and supports thee,
   True in heart, by guile unstainèd;
When He is near nought ever hurts thee,
   E'en when smitten sore and painèd.
   Cross, need, and woe
   He soon averteth,
   O'er the last foe
   His pow'r asserteth.
   Be thou contented!
[203]
How it fareth with thee and others,
   Truly none from Him concealeth,
He ever from on high discovers
   Burden'd hearts, and for them feeleth.
   Of weeping eyes
   The tears He counteth,
   The pile of sighs
   'Fore Him high mounteth.
   Be thou contented!
When not another on earth liveth,
   To whom safe thou may'st confide thee,
He'll faithful prove, who ne'er deceiveth,
   And to happiest end will guide thee.
   The secret grief
   Thy soul that boweth,
   And when relief
   To give, He knoweth.
   Be thou contented!
The sighing of thy soul He ever,
   And thy heart's deep plaint is hear-

ing;
  What to another thou wouldst never
  Tell, reveal to God, ne'er fearing.
[204]
He is not far,
  But standeth near thee,
  Who poor men's pray'r
  Marks, soon will hear thee.
  Be thou contented!
To God cleave, He'll salvation show thee,
  Let not anguish then depress thee;
Although devouring floods o'erflow thee,
  Rise above it, He will bless thee.
  When 'neath the load
  Thy back low bendeth,
  Thy Prince and God
  Soon succour sendeth.
  Be thou contented!
Why for thy life should care so grieve thee,
  How to nourish and sustain it?
Thy God, who ever life doth give thee,
  Will provide for and maintain it.
  He hath a hand
  With gifts o'erflowing,
  On sea and land
  For aye bestowing.
  Be thou contented!
[205]
Who for the forest songsters careth,
  To their daily portion leads them,
For sheep and ox enough prepareth,
  Slakes their thirst, with plenty feeds them;
  He'll care for thee,
  Thee, lone one! filling,
  So bounteously
  Thy hunger stilling.
  Be thou contented!
Say not, the means nowhere appeareth,
  Where I seek, my effort faileth;
God this high name of honour beareth,
  Helper, when no help availeth!
  When thou and I
  Fail to discover
  Him, speedily
  He'll us recover.
  Be thou contented!
Although away thy help is staying,
  He will not for ever leave thee;
Tho' anxious makes thee His delaying,
  'Tis for thy greater good, believe me.
[206]
What on the way
  To come ne'er hasteth,
  Doth longer stay,
  And sweeter tasteth.
  Be thou contented!
Though 'gainst thee hosts of foes are scheming,
  Let not all their lies affright thee;
Still let them rage against thee, deeming
  God will hear it and will right thee.
  Doth God support
  Thee and thine ever?
  The foe can hurt
  Or ruin never.
  Be thou contented!
To each his share of ill is given,
  Would he only see and know it;
No course on earth so fair and even,
  That no trouble lurks below it.
  Who can declare,
  "My house was ever
  All free from care,
  And troubled never?"
  Be thou contented!
[207]
So must it be, in vain our grieving,
  All men here must suffer ever,
  Whate'er upon the earth is living,
  Evil days avoideth never.
  Affliction's blow
  Doth oft depress us,
  And lays us low,
  And death then frees us.
  Be thou contented!
A day will dawn of rest and blessing,
  When our God will come and save us
From the vile body's bands depressing,
  And the evils that enslave us.
  Death soon will come,
  From woe deliver,
  And take us home
  Then all together.
  Be thou contented!
He'll bring us to the hosts in glory,
  To the chosen and true-hearted,
Who when they clos'd this life's sad story,
  Hence in peace to joy departed,
[208]
And on the shore,
  The ever-vernal,
  Hear evermore,
  The voice eternal.
  Be thou contented!

A SONG OF CHRISTIAN CONSOLATION AND JOY.

Is God for me? t'oppose me
  A thousand may uprise;
  When I to pray'r arouse me,
  He'll chase mine enemies.
And doth the Head befriend me,
  Am I belov'd by God?
Let foes then rise to rend me,
  The wild opposing brood!
I know—from faith none moves me,
  I boast—nor feel I shame,
That God as father loves me,
  In Him, a friend I claim.
[209]
Whene'er the tempest rageth,
  At my right hand is He,
  Its violence assuageth,
  And peace restores to me.
My faith securely buildeth
  On Jesus, and His blood;
  This, and this only, yieldeth
  The true eternal good.
The life that my soul liveth,
  Finds nothing on the earth;
What Christ the Saviour giveth
  Of all our love is worth.
My Jesus is my Glory,
  My Splendour, and clear Light,
Liv'd He not in and for me,
  Before God's eye so bright,
And 'fore His pure throne never
  Could I a moment stay,
Must quickly flee for ever,
  As wax 'fore fire away.
[210]
My Jesus death subdueth,
  My sin remitteth quite,
He washeth aad reneweth,
  The crimson maketh white.
I joy in Him, can ever
  A hero's courage feel,
And judgment fear dare never,
  As though uncleansèd still.
Nought, nought, can e'er condemn me,
  My courage take away;
Hell's flames can ne'er o'erwhelm me,
  For me they're quench'd for aye.
No sentence e'er can move me,
  No evil e'er deject,

My Saviour who doth love me,
  Doth with His wings protect.
His Spirit in me dwelleth,
  And ruleth every pow'r,
All pain and sorrow stilleth,
  Dispels all clouds that low'r.
[211]
What He in me implanteth,
  He blesseth every hour,
Help to say "Father" granteth,
  With every ransom'd pow'r.
When heart with terror breaketh,
  And weak and worn I feel,
Words whispers He and speaketh
  That are unspeakable;
My mouth can frame them never,
  To God they are well known,
Who what delights Him ever
  Discovers in His own.
His Spirit mine relieveth
  With words of comfort blest,
Shows how God succour giveth
  To all who seek His rest;
And how a new and golden
  Fair city rear'd hath He,
Which here from sight withholden,
  My joyful eyes shall see.
[212]
My mansion's there so splendid,
  Prepar'd in yonder land;
Though when my course is ended,
  I fall—Heav'n still doth stand.
Though care here often saddens
  And causeth tears to flow,
My Jesu's light oft gladdens
  And sweetens every woe.
Whoe'er to Jesus bindeth
  Himself, doth Satan hate,
He's troubled much and findeth
  His burden sore and great;
To suffer scarce is able,
  Disgrace and scorn he meets,
The cross and every trouble
  As daily bread he eats.
My mind this clear perceiveth,
  Yet am I undismay'd;
To Thee my heart aye cleaveth,
  On Thee shall cares be laid.
[213]
Though life and limb it cost me
  And everything I have,
Unshaken shall I trust Thee,
  Thee never shall I leave.
The world may ruin shiver,
  Thou liv'st eternally,

Nor sword nor flame shall ever
  Divide 'twixt Thee and me.
No thirst nor gnawing hunger,
  No pain nor poverty,
Nor mighty prince's anger
  Shall ever hinder me.
No angel, nought that gladdens,
  No throne nor majesty,
No love nor aught that saddens,
  No grief nor misery,
Nor aught that man discovers,
  Be it small or great,
From Thee, my heav'nly Lover's
  Embrace can separate.
[214]
My heart with joy is springing,
  And sad I cannot be,
'Tis full of joy and singing,
  The sunshine doth it see.
The Sun that looks with pleasure
  On me is Christ my King;
The glory beyond measure
  That waits me, makes me sing.

A SONG OF CHRISTIAN JOY.

Why should sorrow ever grieve me?
  Christ is near,
  What can here
  E'er of Him deprive me?
Who can rob me of my heaven
  That God's Son,
  As mine own,
  To my faith hath given?
[215]
Naked was I and unswathèd
  When on earth
  At my birth
  My first breath I breathèd.
Naked hence shall I betake me,
  When I go
  From earth's woe,
  And my breath forsake me.
Nought—not e'en the life I'm living,
  Is mine own,
  God alone
  All to me is giving.
Must I then His own restore Him?
  Though bereft
  Of each gift
  Still shall I adore Him.
Though a heavy cross I'm bearing,
  And my heart
  Feels the smart,
  Shall I be despairing?
[216]
God can help me, who doth send it,

  He doth know
  All my woe
  And how best to end it.
God oft gives me days of gladness,
  Shall I grieve
  If He give
  Seasons too of sadness?
God is good, and tempers ever
  Every hurt,
  Me desert
  Wholly can He never,
Though united world and devil,
  All their pow'r
  Can no more
  Do than mock and cavil.
Let derision now employ them,
  Christ e'en here
  Will appear
  And 'fore all destroy them.
[217]
True believers shrinking never,
  Where they dwell
  Should reveal
  Their true colours ever.
When approaching death would scare them,
  Still should they
  Patient stay
  And with courage bear them.
Death can never kill us even,
  But relief
  From all grief
  To us then is given.
It doth close life's mournful story,
  Make a way
  That we may
  Pass to heav'nly glory.
There I'll reap enduring pleasure,
  After woe
  Here below
  Suffer'd in large measure.
[218]
Lasting good we find here never,
  All the earth
  Deemeth worth
  Vanisheth for ever.
What is all this life possesseth?
  But a hand
  Fall of sand
  That the heart distresseth.
Noble gifts that pall me never,
  Christ so free
  There gives me
  To enjoy for ever.
Shepherd! Lord! joy's fountain ever,

Thou art mine,
I am Thine,
No one can us sever.
I am Thine, because Thou gavest
Life and blood
For my good,
By Thy death me savest.
[219]
Thou'rt mine, for I love and own Thee,
  Ne'er shall I,
  Light of joy,
  From my heart dethrone Thee.
Let me, let me soon behold Thee
  Face to face,
  Thy embrace
  May it soon enfold me!

CHRISTIAN DEVOTION TO GOD'S WILL.

I into God's own heart and mind
  My heart and mind deliver,
What evil seems, a gain I find,
  E'en death is life for ever.
I am His son,
Who spread the throne
Of heaven high above me.
Tho' I bend low
Beneath His blow,
Yet still His heart doth love me.
[220]
He ne'er can prove untrue to me,
  My Father aye must love me,
And tho' He cast me in the sea,
  He only thus would prove me;
In what He good
Doth count, He would
My heart establish ever.
And if I stand,
His mighty hand
Will raise me, and deliver.
Vain had my own pow'r ever been,
  To have adorn'd or made me;
In soul and body God is seen,
  He form'd and He array'd me,
Plac'd mind and wit
On the soul's seat,
And flesh and bones did give me.
Who thus so free
Supplieth me
Can ne'er mean to deceive me.
[221]
Say, where a place to lay my head,
  On earth had I attainèd?
  Long since had I been cold and dead
  Had God not me sustainèd
With His strong arm,
That ever warm,
And glad and healthy maketh.
Whom He gives joy
May praise employ,
What He leaves, falls and breaketh.
Wisdom and understanding true
  In Him are ever dwelling;
Time, place, to leave undone or do,
  He knoweth, never failing.
He ever knows
When joys, when woes,
Are best for those He loveth.
What He doth here—
Tho' it appear
Ill—to be good aye proveth.
[222]
Thou think'st indeed, if thou hast not
  What flesh and blood is yearning
  To have, that trial mars thy lot,
  Thy light to darkness turning.
Of toil and care
Thou hast large share,
Ere thou thy wish attainest,
And dost not see
Whatever thee
Befals, thereby thou gainest.
In truth, He who created thee,
  His glory in thee showing,
Hath long ago in His decree
  Determin'd—all foreknowing—
What good for thee
And thine will be,
In faithfulness he'll give it.
Curb thou thy will,
Wait! be thou still,
To His good pleasure leave it.
[223]
Whate'er to send, seems good to God,
  'Twill be at last refreshing,
Altho' thou call'st it cross and load
  'Tis fraught with richest blessing.
Wait patiently,
His grace to thee
He'll speedily discover.
All grief and fear
Shall disappear
Like mist the hills spread over.
The field, unless the storm rage high,
  Its ripe fruits yieldeth never,
So men were ruin'd utterly
  If all were prosp'rous ever.
Though health it gives,
And thus relieves,
The bitter aloe paineth;
So must the heart
With anguish smart,
Ere it to health attaineth.
[224]
My God! my God! into Thy hand
  I joyfully now yield me,
Keep me, a stranger in the land,
  E'en to the end, Lord! shield me.
Deal with me now
As well dost know,
That I may profit by it;
Then more and more
Thy glorious pow'r,
Lord! show, and magnify it.
Wilt cause Thy sun on me to shine,
  With pleasure, Lord, I'll share it;
Should trial or mischance be mine,
  Then patiently I'll bear it.
Of life the door
Should it before
Me open here stand ever,
Where Thou lead'st me,
I'll joyfully
Go with Thee, shrinking never.
[225]
Should I along the path of death,
  Through the dark vale be treading,
'Tis well, 'tis the appointed path,
  E'en there Thine eyes are leading.
My Shepherd! Thou
Art all below
To such an issue bringing,
That I to Thee,
Eternally,
Shall songs of praise be singing.

COMMIT THY WAY UNTO THE LORD, TRUST ALSO IN HIM, AND HE SHALL BRING IT TO PASS.—PSALM XXXVII. 5.

Commit whatever grieves thee
  At heart, and all thy ways,
To Him who never leaves thee,
  On whom creation stays.
Who freest courses maketh
For clouds, and air, and wind,
And care who ever taketh
A path for thee to find.
[226]
The Lord thou must repose on
  If thou wouldst prosper sure,
His work must ever gaze on
  If thine is to endure.
By anxious care and grieving,
By self-consuming pain,
God is not mov'd to giving;
By pray'r must thou obtain.

Thy grace that ever floweth,
  O Father! what is good,
Or evil, ever knoweth,
  To mortal flesh and blood.
What to Thine eye all-seeing,
  And to Thy counsel wise
Seems good, doth into being,
  O mighty Prince, arise!
For means it fails Thee never,
  Thou always find'st a way,
Thy doing's blessing ever,
  Thy path like brightest day.
[227]
Thy work can no one hinder,
  Thy labour cannot rest,
If Thou design'st Thy tender
  Children should be bless'd.
Though all the powers of evil
  Should rise up to resist,
Without a doubt or cavil
  God never will desist;
His undertakings ever
  At length He carries through;
What He designs He never
  Can fail at all to do.
Hope on, thou heart, grief-riven,
  Hope, and courageous be,
Where anguish thee hath driven,
  Thou shalt deliv'rance see.
God, from thy pit of sadness
  Shall raise thee graciously;
Wait, and the sun of gladness
  Thine eyes shall early see.
[228]
Up! up! to pain and anguish
  A long good night now say;
Drive all that makes thee languish
  In grief and woe away.
Thine 'tis not to endeavour
  The ruler's part to play,
God sits as ruler ever,
  Guides all things well each day.
Let Him alone—and tarry
  He is a Prince all wise,
He shall Himself so carry,
  'Twill strange seem in thine eyes,
When He as Him beseemeth,
  In wonderful decree,
Shall as Himself good deemeth,
  O'errule what grieveth thee.
He may awhile still staying
  His comforts keep from thee,
And on His part delaying,
  Seem to have utterly
[229]

Forgotten and forsaken
  And put thee out of mind,
Though thou'rt by grief o'ertaken,
  No time for thee to find.
But if thou never shrinkest,
  And true dost still remain,
He'll come when least thou thinkest,
  And set thee free again,
Thee from the load deliver,
  That burdeneth thy heart,
That thou hast carried never
  For any evil part.
Hail! child of faith, who gainest
  The victory alway,
Who honour's crown obtainest,
  That never fades away.
God in thy hand will give thee,
  One day, the glorious palm;
Who ne'er in grief did leave thee,
  To Him thou'lt sing thy psalm.
[230]
O Lord no longer lengthen
  Our time of misery,
Our hands and feet now strengthen,
  And until death may we
By Thee be watched and car'd for,
  In faithfulness and love,
So come we where prepar'd for
  Us is our bless'd abode.

SONG OF CONSOLATION.

Thou must not altogether be
  O'ercome by sad vexation,
God soon will cause to shine on thee
  The light of consolation.
In patience wait, and be thou still,
And let the Lord do what He will,
  He never can do evil.
[231]
Is this the first time we have known
  And tasted sore affliction?
What have we had but grief alone
  On earth, and sore dejection?
We've had an ample share of grief,
Yet God hath sometimes sent relief,
  A respite brief of gladness.
Not so doth God our Father mean,
  When His afflictions grieve us,
That no more shall His face be seen
  That He'll for ever leave us;
His purposes quite other are,
That those who from Him wander far
  By trial be recover'd.
It is our nature's evil mood
  That when in joys we're living,
We then forsake our highest good,

  Ourselves to license giving.
We earthly are, and deem more worth
The things and pleasures of the earth,
  Than all that dwells in heaven.
[232]
God therefore all our joys doth blight,
  Lets trials overtake us,
Takes that wherein our hearts delight,
  Look up to Him to make us,
That to His goodness and His pow'r,
That we've neglected heretofore,
  We may return as children.
When we return to Him again
  He graciously receives us,
To joy He turns our every pain,
  To laughter turns what grieves us;
To Him it is a simple art,
He soon doth help to him impart
  Whom He with love embraceth.
Afflicted band! oh, fall ye now
  With contrite hearts before Him,
Tell Him that ye in homage bow
  To His great name; implore Him
In grace your sins to take away,
The load He on your backs did lay
  To bear, your wounds to bind up.
[233]
Grace always before right must go,
  And wrath to love yield ever;
His merest mercy, when we low
  Are lying, must deliver.
His hand it is upholds us all,
If we let go, then break and fall
  Must all our work to pieces.
On God's love must thou ever stay,
  Nor let aught overthrow thee,
E'en when the heav'ns shall pass away
  And earth shall crash below thee:
God promiseth His grace to thee,
His word is clear, who fearlessly
  Trusts it, is ne'er deceivèd.
So darest thou His pow'r so great
  Ne'er doubt a moment even,
Who is it that doth all create,—
  By whom all gifts are given?
God doth it, and His counsel wise
Can ever ways and means devise,
  When every man despaireth.
[234]
Seems help impossible to thee?
  This should'st thou know however,
God by our narrow thoughts can be
  Hemm'd and confinèd never,
This ne'er to us alloweth He;

He everywhere,—His arm is free,—
  Doth more than we can fathom.
What is His wide dominion fair?
  'Tis full of varied wonder;
He helpeth us when dark despair
  We helplessly sink under,
To His great name this is the praise,
If thou wilt see His holy place,
  Thou must ascribe for ever.

[235]

THE 13TH PSALM OF DAVID.

How long, Lord, in forgetfulness
  And darkness wilt Thou leave me?
How long will sorrow on me press
  And deep heart-anguish grieve me?
Wilt Thou Thy face, Lord, utterly
Turn from me? wilt ne'er look on me
  In grace and in compassion?
How long shall I, thy stricken child,
  Bereft of soul-rest languish?
How long shall storm and wind so wild,
  Fill heart with fear and anguish?
How long shall my proud enemy,
  Who only meaneth ill to me,
  Exult o'er me in triumph?
Ah! look on me, my Shield and Lord!
  Down from Thy holy heaven,
  And hear now my complaining word,
  My pray'r from heart grief-riven.
  Give to mine eyes, Lord, pow'r and might,
  And do not let death's gloomy night
  So speedily o'ertake me.

[236]

For then, Lord, ev'ry enemy
  Would never cease to glory,
  And were I prostrate utterly,
  Would ever triumph o'er me.
"There lieth he," they'd cry in joy,
"Who caus'd us evermore annoy,
  He's prostrate and ne'er riseth."
I know them, and I know fall well
  The wickedness they're planning,
  Their hearts with ev'ry evil swell,
  No good them e'er restraining.
But Thou, the faithful One, Lord, art,
  And those who choose Thee for their part,
  Thou nevermore forsakest.
My soul doth calmly trust in Thee,
  Thou true to me remainest,
  Of malice and of subtlety
  The course, with pow'r restrainest.
  This makes my heart with joy o'erflow,
  That willingly dost Thou bestow
  Salvation on the trusting.

[237]

O Lord! for aye I'll trust in Thee,
  Thou'rt my sole joy for ever;
  Thou doest well, protectest me,
  From sorrow dost deliver.
  And therefore I my whole life long,
  Will sing Thee oft a gladsome song
  Of praise and of thanksgiving.

Songs of Praise and Thanksgiving.

[238]

IN GRATEFUL SONGS.

In grateful songs your voices raise,
  All people here below,
  To Him whom angels ever praise,
  In heav'n His glory show.
With gladsome songs now fill the air
  To God our chiefest Joy,
  Who worketh wonders ev'rywhere,
  Whose hands great things employ;
Who from the womb to latest years
  Upholds the life He gave;
  Who when no help from man appears
  Himself appears to save;

[239]

Who though our way His heart oft grieves,
  Maintains a gracious mood,
  Remits the pains, the sin forgives,
  And doth us nought but good.
Oh, may He give a joyous heart,
  The mind from sorrow keep,
  And cast all care, fear, grief, and smart
  Into the ocean deep.
And may His blessing ever rest
  On Israel's favour'd head;
  May all we do by Him be bless'd,
  May His salvation spread.
May love and goodness toward us flow,
  In bounteous streams each day,
  And every anxious care we know,
  Be chas'd by Him away.
As long as beats each throbbing heart,
  Our Saviour may He be,
  Our portion when from earth we part,
  To all eternity.

[240]

When sinks the heart, when strength decays,
  By Him our eyes be press'd,
  Then may we see His open face,
  In everlasting rest.

SHALL I NOT MY GOD BE PRAISING?

Shall I not my God be praising,
  And in Him not joyful be?
For in all His works amazing,
  See I not His care for me?
Is it not pure love that filleth,
  And His faithful heart o'erflows,
  When He ever cares for those,
  Who do only what He willeth?
All things run their course below,
God's love doth for ever flow.

[241]

As its brood the eagle over,
  Ever more its wings doth spread.
So the Highest aye doth cover
  With His arms of pow'r my head.
In the womb e'en of my mother,
  When to me He being gave,
  E'en the life that now I have,
  Was He then my shield and cover.
All things run their course below,
God's love doth for ever flow.
Not too great a gift He even
  Deem'd His only Son to be;
  Him to death hath freely given,
  Me from fear of hell to free.
Oh! Thou spring of boundless blessing,
  How could e'er my feeble mind
  Of Thy depth the bottom find,
  Though my efforts were unceasing?
All things run their course below,
God's love doth for ever flow.

[242]

And the Holy Ghost to guide me,
  Noble Leader! He hath giv'n,
  That He through the world may lead me,
  Onward to the gate of heav'n.
  That my heart He may be filling
  With th' unclouded light of faith,
  That can break the pow'r of death,
  And hell's rage hath pow'r of stilling.
All things run their course below,
God's love doth for ever flow.
For my soul's well-being ever
  Full provision doth He make,
  And in ev'ry need deliver,
  For the body care doth take.
When my pow'r, my best endeavour
  Cometh to extremity,
  Then my God appears to me,
  With His might comes to deliver.

All things run their course below,
  God's love doth for ever flow.
[243]
All the things in earth and heaven,
  E'en where'er I turn my eye,
  For my benefit are given,
  That they may my need supply.
All that's living, all that's growing,
  On the hills or in the woods,
  In the vales or 'neath the floods,
  God is for my good bestowing.
All things run their course below,
  God's love doth for ever flow.
When I sleep, His eye is waking,
  When I wake, He strength'neth me,
  Each new morn fresh courage taking,
  I new love and goodness see.
Had my God existed never,
  Had His face not guided me,
  From such ills so frequently,
  None could have deliver'd ever.
All things run their course below,
  God's love doth for ever flow.
[244]
'Gainst me many is the weapon,
  Forg'd by Satan's enmity,
  But no real hurt can happen,
  None hath yet befallen me.
God's own angel whom He sendeth,
  Wardeth off each deadly blow
  Aim'd by the untiring foe,
  Who our ruin thus intendeth.
All things run their course below,
  God's love doth for ever flow.
As a father ne'er withdraweth
  From his child his love away,
  Though he often evil doeth,
  And from wisdom's paths doth stray.
So God's heart towards me moveth,
  All my sins forgiveth He,
  Not in vengeance smiteth me,
  As a Father He reproveth.
All things run their course below,
  God's love doth for ever flow.
[245]
Ev'ry blow His hand inflicteth,
  Though the heart with pain it rend,
  When my heart aright reflecteth,
  Is a token that my Friend
Thinks on me, and tow'rds me yearneth,
  Me from this ill world would free,
  That has so entangled me,
  By the cross to Him me turneth.
All things run their course below,
  God's love doth for ever flow.
This I know full well, and never
  Let it from my mind depart,
  Christ's cross hath its limit ever,
  And at length must cease to smart.
When the winter snows are over
  Lovely summer will appear,
  Who can hope, from ev'ry fear,
  And from pain, shall they recover.
All things run their course below,
  God's love doth for ever flow.
[246]
In God's love there is no ending,
  Ne'er a limit find I there,
  So my hands to Thee extending,
  As Thy child, I raise my pray'r.
Father! deign Thy grace to give me,
  That I may with all my might
  Thee embrace both day and night,
  All my life may never leave thee,
  And when life is o'er with me,
  Love and praise eternally.

PROTECTION OF GOD IN HITHERTO DANGEROUS TIMES OF WAR.

How heavy is the burden made
  That Thou upon our backs hast laid,
  O God! the Lord of Hosts,
  O God, whose anger rises high
  'Gainst workers of iniquity.
[247]
The burden is the cruel tide
  Of war, that earth with blood has dyed,
  And fill'd with bitter tears.
  It is a fire that rages high
  'Neath suns of almost every sky.
The burden's great and hard to bear,
  But Thy strong arm and Father's care
  Are not to us unknown.
  Thou punishest, but 'mid the woe
  Thou love and friendliness dost show.
But true to Thee must we abide,
  For ne'er from us dost Thou quite hide
  Thy saving health and light.
  How many hast Thou given o'er,
  We've oft been shielded by Thy pow'r.
In many a sad and weary hour,
  When gath'ring clouds did o'er us low'r
  Above our anxious heads,
  Thou still'd'st the storm, whose mighty hand
  Upholdeth sky and sea and land.
[248]
How often, Lord, by day and night,
  Our enemies with craft and might
  Have threaten'd us, Thy flock!
  But, faithful Shepherd! Thou wast near,
  Repell'dst the wolf and still'dst our fear.
Our brethren are compell'd to roam,
  Are driven forth from house and home,
  While we, Lord, still enjoy
  Each one his seat beneath the shade
  By his own vine and fig-tree made.
Behold! my heart, on every hand
  The towns and fields of many a land
  Are doom'd to ruin sure,
  The homes of men are overthrown,
  The houses of our God cast down.
But rest and order still remain
  With us, and we can still maintain
  The worship of our God.
  God's mind from out His holy word
  'Mongst us is daily taught and heard.
[249]
Whoever this doth not perceive,
  But to the winds such thoughts doth give,
  Who in such blessèd light
  No grace, no love, no goodness find,
  How dark, thrice darken'd is their mind!
O gracious God! preserve us free
  For aye from such stupidity;
  Lord, give us gratitude,
  That songs of praise in sweetest tone
  We may present before Thy throne.
To nought we've done, or e'er can do,
  To Thee—to Thee alone is due
  The praise, O fount of love!
  We've earn'd destruction from Thy face,
  Thou deal'st with us in love and grace.
Oh! may we meditate Thy grace,
  Till heart shall burn and tongue shall praise,
  And give angelic zeal,
  That every throbbing pulse may be
  A note of praise, O Lord! to Thee.
[250]
But let the tide of woe recede,
  Restore to us our joy, we plead,

May peace to us return.
How many in this vale of tears
Have never witness'd peaceful years!
Are we unworthy? then with Thee
  We plead for helpless infancy,
  Who wrong have never done.
  Shall cradled infants feel the stroke,
  Shall they endure the heavy yoke?
Have pity, Lord! oh, tender heart!
  What heavy sighs, what bitter smart,
  From our sad hearts are wrung!
  No stone, our Saviour God art Thou,
  How canst Thou so afflict us now?
How grievous are our wounds and sore,
  They stink and fester more and more,
  But Thou canst heal them all.
  Pour in the oil of grace, that whole
  Can make the body and the soul.
[251]
This wilt Thou do, we certainly
  Believe, although we nowhere see
  The means in all the world.
  But Thou in our extremity
  Dost find Thine opportunity.

THANKSGIVING FOR THE DECLARATION OF PEACE.

Praise God! for forth hath sounded
  The noble word of joy and peace,
  There's rest where strife abounded,
  The sword and spear their murders cease.
  Up! up! again, and bring ye
  Now forth the sounding lyre,
  O Germany! and sing ye
  In full and noble choir,
  Your hearts and minds now raise ye
  And thank the Lord, and say,
  "Thy grace and goodness praise we
  For they endure for aye!"
[252]
'Twere just if God were driving
  Us in dire wrath from 'fore His face,
  For with us still are thriving
  The thorns of sin that grow apace.
  In deed and truth we feel it—
  His rod of chastisement!
  But say whoe'er can tell it—
  Who are they who repent?
  We're only evil ever,
  God's true continually,
  He helpeth to deliver
  From war and misery.
With grateful hearts o'erflowing
  We greet thee, noble gift of peace!
  Where'er thou dwell'st, now knowing
  How richly thou dost ever bless.
  God to thy keeping giveth
  Our good and happiness,
  Who woundeth thee and grieveth,
  In his own heart doth press
[253]
Grief's arrow, and in madness
  He quencheth in the land
  The golden light of gladness
  With suicidal hand.
What could this lesson ever
  Grave on our hearts so solemnly,
  As forts laid low for ever,
  And towns that now in ruins lie:
  As fair and fertile meadows
  That wav'd with golden grain,
  Now wrapt in forest shadows
  And run to waste again.
  As graves full of the buried,
  Who fell in the dread hour
  Of battle in ranks serried,
  Whose like we'll see no more.
O man! be now afflicted,
  And let thy tears in torrents flow,
  With countenance dejected
  To ponder to thy closet go;
[254]
What heretofore hath given
  Thy God, didst thou deride,
  Thy Father who's in Heaven
  Now turn'd hath to thy side.
  From fury and from pressing
  He turneth for thy good,
  As if by love and blessing
  Constrain thy heart He would.
Awake thee! now awake thee!
  Thou hard, cold world awaken'd be;
  Ere doom's dread hour o'ertake thee,
  By thee unlook'd for, suddenly.
  Ye for the Saviour living!
  Unshaken be your mood,
  The peace He now is giving
  Can only bring us good.
  This lesson He is giving,
  The end of all is nigh,
  Thou shalt with Him be living
  In peace eternally.
[255]

O LORD! I SING WITH MOUTH AND HEART.

O Lord! I sing with mouth and heart,
  Joy of my soul! to Thee
  To earth Thy knowledge I impart,
  As it is known to me.
Thou art the Fount of grace, I know,
  And Spring aye fall and free,
  Whence saving health and goodness flow
  Each day so bounteously.
What have we here or what are we,
  Of good what can earth give,
  That we do not alone from Thee,
  Our Father, aye receive?
The tent-like firmament who builds,
  Who spreads th' expanse of blue,
  Who sends to fertilize our fields
  Refreshing rain and dew?
[256]
Who warmeth us in cold and frost,
  Who shields us from the wind,
  Who orders it that wine and must
  We in their season find?
Who is it life and health bestows,
  Who keeps us with His hand
  In golden peace, wards off war's woes,
  From our dear native land?
The work is Thine, my God! my Lord!
  And Thine must ever be;
  Before our door Thou keepest guard,
  In rest we're kept by Thee.
Thou feedest us from year to year,
  And constant dost abide;
  When danger fills our hearts with fear,
  With help art at our side.
With patience dost Thou ever chide,
  Nor long Thine anger keep,
  But castest all our sins aside
  Into the ocean deep.
[257]
Whene'er our burden'd hearts we raise
  To Thee, Thou'rt soon appeas'd;
  The help Thou send'st shows forth Thy praise,
  And our sad hearts are eas'd.
Thou mark'st how oft Thy people weep
  And what their sorrows are,
  Their tears dost in Thy bottle keep,
  However small they are.
Our deepest needs dost Thou supply,
  Thou giv'st what lasts for aye,
  Thou lead'st us to our home on high,
  When hence we pass away.
Awake! my heart, awake and sing,
  And joyous be thy mood,
  Thy God who maketh everything
  Is, and abides thy good—
Thy treasure and inheritance!

Thy glory and delight!
  Thy saving health and sure defence!
  He keeps and guides thee right.
[258]
Why do thy cares both night and day
  Grieve thee so bitterly?
  Upon thy God thy burden lay,
  Who gave thy life to thee.
Hath He not all the weary way
  From youth till now thee led,
  Oft chas'd misfortune's clouds away
  That gather'd o'er thy head?
In all His rule no oversight
  Can happen, no mistakes;
  Whate'er He does or leaves is right,
  A happy issue takes.
Let Him work who doth all things well,
  Nor with Him interfere,
  And so thou shalt in glory dwell,
  And peace enjoy while here.
[259]

TO GOD ALONE BE GLORY.

How can it be, my highest Light!
  That as before Thy face so bright
  All things must pale and vanish,
  That my poor feeble flesh and blood
  Can summon a courageous mood
  To meet Thee, and fear banish?
But dust and ashes what am I?
  My body what but grass so dry?
  What good the life I'm living?
  What can I with my utmost pow'r?
  What have I, Lord! from hour to hour
  But what Thyself art giving?
I am a poor and feeble worm,
  A straw, the lightest passing storm
  Could drive away before it.
  When Thou Thy hand, that all doth stay,
  Dost on me e'er so lightly lay,
  I know not how t' endure it.
[260]
Lord! I am nought, but Thou art He
  Who art all—all belongs to Thee,
  And live and move I ever
  In Thee—if Thou me terrifi'st,
  No store of grace to help suppli'st
  I can recover never.
I am unjust, but true Thy heart,
  I evil am—Thou holy art,
  This thought should shame be giving,
  That I in such an evil stand,
  Should from Thy mild paternal hand,
  The least good be receiving.
Nought else but ill from infancy
Up e'en till now I've done to Thee,
  In sin was I begotten;
  And didst Thou not in faithfulness
  My sin remit, and me release,
  Lost were I and forgotten.
Let boasting then be far from me,
  What is Thy due I render Thee,
[261]
To Thee alone be glory!
  O Christ! may while I live below
  My spirit, and what thence may flow,
  With reverence adore Thee.
And if aught hath been done by me
  That is well done, it came from Thee,
  My pow'r could do it never.
Thee thanks and honour, Lord! I bring,
  All my life long Thy praise I'll sing,
  And tell Thy glory ever.

SONG OF THANKSGIVING AFTER GREAT SORROW AND AFFLICTION.

After clouds we see the sun,
  Joy we feel when grief is gone,
  After bitter pain and sore
  Cometh consolation's hour.
  Then my soul that sank before,
  Even down to hell's dark door,
  To the heav'nly choir doth soar.
[262]
He 'fore whom the world shall flee,
  In my spirit comforts me,
  With His high and mighty hand,
  Tears me from the hellish band.
  With the love to me He shows,
  Swells my heart and overflows,
  And my blood with rapture glows.
Did I e'er 'neath sorrow bend?
  Did my heart grief ever rend?
  Have I e'er been vexèd sore?
  Satan e'er fool'd me before?
  Aye—but henceforth am I free,
  Faithfully thou shieldest me,
  My salvation comes from Thee!
What thou mean'st, my bitter foe!
  By thy deeds tow'rds me I know;
  Truly thou with all thy pow'r
  Seek'st me ever to devour.
  Had I too much trusted thee,
  Then had'st thou, ere I could see,
  In thy snares entangled me.
[263]
All the guile I know full well
  That in thy bad heart doth dwell;
  Thou my God malign'st to me,
  Turn'st His praise to obloquy;
  Speaketh out His loving heart,
  Keeps He silence on His part,
  All He doth dost thou pervert.
If I hope and look for good,
  If I'm in a joyous mood,
  From my mind thou driv'st away
  Every good thought—and dost say:
  "God doth far from thee abide,
  Riseth high misfortune's tide
  Round thee now on every side."
Hence depart! thou lying mouth,
  Here is God's own ground in truth,
  For the face of God is here,
  And the beauteous light and clear
  Of His favour, here doth rise,
  All His word and counsel wise,
  Op'd are now before mine eyes.
[264]
God lets none in sadness stay,
  He with shame drives none away,
  Who themselves up to Him give,
  With the whole heart to Him cleave,
  Who their cares on Him aye cast,
  And hope in Him—joy at last,
  For the soul and body taste.
Though it comes not as we will,
  Just to-day—yet be thou still,
  For perchance to-morrow may
  Be the bright and joyous day.
  God's time comes with measur'd step,
  When it comes His word He'll keep
  And joy's harvest we shall reap.
Ah! how often did I think,
  As my feet began to sink
  'Neath the heavy load of care,
  In the mire of blank despair,
  Now there is no hope for me,
  Rest for me there cannot be
  Till I enter death's dark sea.
[265]
But my God put forth His pow'r
  To avert and to restore,
  That I ne'er enough can tell
  What His arm hath done so well;
  When no path I could descry,
  When no help to guide was nigh,
  Help God sent me from on high.
When I timid and perplex'd
  Often have my spirit vex'd,
  Sleepless toss'd thro' all the night,
  Sick at heart when dawn'd the light,
  When heart fail'd me utterly,
  Hast Thou then appear'd to me,

Turning my captivity.
Now as long as here I roam,
   Have on earth a house and home,
   'Fore mine eyes continually
   Shall this thing of wonder be.
   All my life long shall I bring
   Offerings of thanks, and sing
   Songs of praise to God my King.
[266]
Every grief and every smart,
   By th'eternal Father's heart
   Ever yet appointed me,
   Or that may hereafter be
   Chosen for me, all my days
   From His gracious hand always,
   I'll receive with joy and praise.
I will tread woe's bitter path,
   I will onward go to death,
   I into the grave will go,
   Still my heart with joy shall glow.
   Whom the Highest will raise high,
   Whom th' Almighty standeth nigh,
   Ne'er can perish utterly.

THE 23RD PSALM OF DAVID.

The Lord, the earth who ruleth,
   And with His hand controlleth,
   Whose goodness never endeth,
   He watcheth me and tendeth.
[267]
As long as He is near me
   With every gift He'll cheer me,
   Of fulness overflowing
   The riches aye bestowing.
By pastures green He leads me,
   With gladness there He feeds me,
   From purest springs revives me,
   In need He counsel gives me.
And when the soul is fearful
   Through grievous thoughts and careful,
   He comfort giveth ever
   And knows how to deliver.
My steps aright He leadeth,
   And what to do me guideth,
   And for His name's sake glorious
   O'er fear makes me victorious.
Though often left to ponder,
   While in dark vales I wander,
   No evil fear I ever,
   Distress o'ertakes me never.
[268]
Thou standest still beside me,
   From wicked men dost hide me,
   Thy rod and staff protect me,
   And no fear can deject me.
My table Thou preparest,
   For my refreshment carest,
   When foes are plotting round me,
   And seek to pain and wound me.
My head with oil anointest,
   My empty soul appointest
   Of every good and pleasure
   A full o'erflowing measure.
The goodness Thou bestowest,
   The mercy that Thou showest,
   Till life itself forsake me,
   Shall glad and joyful make me.
Thy service will I never
   Forsake, but praise Thee ever,
   In Thy house where Thou livest,
   Reward to goodness givest.
[269]
As long as life is given
   On earth here, and in heaven
   Where I shall stand before Thee,
   I'll evermore adore Thee!

Morning and Evening Songs.
[270]

MORNING BLESSING.

The golden morning,
   Joy her adorning,
   With splendour near us
   Draweth, to cheer us
With her heart-refreshing and lovely light.
   My head and members
   Lay wrapt all in slumbers,
   But now awaking,
   And sleep from me shaking,
   Heaven's bless'd sunshine doth gladden my sight.
Mine eye beholdeth
   What God upholdeth,
   Made for His glory,
   To tell the story
[271]
To us of His power and might so great,
   And where the Father
   The faithful shall gather
   In peace, whenever
   Earth's lies they shall sever
And leave this mortal and perishing state.
Come ye with singing,
   To God be bringing
   Goods and each blessing—
   All we're possessing—
All be to God as an offering brought.
   Hearts with love glowing,
   With praises o'erflowing,
   Thanksgiving voices,
   In these God rejoices,
All other off'rings without them are nought.
To morn and even
   His thoughts are given,
   Increase He giveth,
   Sorrow relieveth,
[272]
These are the works that He doeth alone.
   When we are sleeping
   Watch is He aye keeping,
   When we're awaking
   Care still of us taking,
He makes the light of His grace to shine down.
My thoughts I've raisèd
   To Thee who'rt praisèd
   For aye in Heaven!
   Success be given,
May all my endeavours unhinder'd be!
   From ev'ry evil
   And work of the devil,
   All malice ever,
   Oh do Thou deliver!
In all Thy precepts establish Thou me!
May't pleasure give me,
   May no pain grieve me
   To see flow over
   The cup my brother
[273]
Or neighbour hath, with Thy blessings so free.
   Covetous burning
   And unchristian yearning
   For ill possessions,
   Blot out such transgressions,
   Cast them, O Father! all into the sea!
The life we're living
   What is it giving?
   Ere any thinketh
   To ground it sinketh,
Soon as the breath of the grave on it blow.
   All things together
   Dread ruin must shiver,
   The earth and heaven
   They must perish even,
Wrapt in the flames that shall ardently glow!
All—all decayeth,

But God still stayeth,
His thoughts they waver
A moment never,
[274]
His word and will both eternally 'dure.
His grace and favour
Uninjur'd are ever,
Deadly wounds healing,
The heart with peace filling,
Health here and yonder to us they ensure.
My God for ever
Do Thou deliver!
Shield me, and cover
My debts all over,
In grace, Thine eyes from my sins turn away.
Govern and guide me,
Be ever beside me,
As it is pleasing
To Thee! am I placing
All in Thy hand and disposal for aye.
Wilt Thou give ever
To me whatever
My life is needing?
May I be heeding
[275]
Ever the faithful word spoken by Thee.
God is the highest,
The greatest, the nighest,
Gracious is ever,
Is changeable never,
Of all our treasures the noblest is He.
Wilt Thou then grieve me,
Gall to drink give me?
Must I be passing
Through cares harassing?
Do then as seemeth it good unto Thee.
Whate'er supporteth,
Is useful or hurteth,
Thou knowest ever,
And chastenest never
Too much, in case we o'erburden'd should be.
Trial God sendeth,
Speedily endeth
The storms of ocean,
The wind's commotion
[276]
Lightens the sunshine so gladsome and bright.
Fulness of pleasure,
And glorious leisure,
Will then be given
To me in yon Heaven
Whither my thoughts aye to turn take delight.

AWAKE, MY HEART!

Awake, my heart! be singing,
  Praise to thy Maker bringing,
  Of every good the Giver,
  Who men protecteth ever.
As shades of night spread over
  Earth as a pall did cover,
  Then Satan sought to have me,
  But God was near to save me.
[277]
When Satan would devour me,
  Thou, Father! spreadest o'er me
  Thy wing, Thou me embraced'st,
  All fear away Thou chased'st.
Thou said'st "Lie still, I'm near thee;
  In spite of him who'd tear thee,
  Sleep, child! let nought affright thee,
  The sunlight shall delight thee."
Thou truly, Lord! hast told it,
  The light—mine eyes behold it,
  From dangers hast releas'd me,
  Thou hast renew'd and bless'd me.
Thou sacrifice would'st ever,
  My gifts I bring Thee hither,
  The offerings I'm bringing
  My pray'rs are and my singing.
Such Thou disdainest never,
  The heart Thou can'st search ever,
  Thou know'st none can deceive Thee
  No better can I give Thee.
[278]
Thou wilt, O Lord! be ending
  Thy work in me, and sending
  Who in his hands will take me,
  To-day his care will make me.
May I in all I'm doing
  Wise courses be pursuing,
  Beginning, middle, ending,
  May all to bliss be tending.
Thy blessings richly give me,
  My heart would now receive Thee,
  Thy word as food be given
  To me till I reach Heaven.
[279]

PRAISE YE JEHOVAH!

Praise ye Jehovah,
  All ye men who fear Him!
  Let us with gladness to His name be singing,
  Be thanks and praises to His altar bringing.
Praise ye Jehovah!
The life we're living
  Who is ever giving;
  Care all the night who like a father taketh,
  And who with gladness us from sleep awaketh.
Praise ye Jehovah!
That we enjoy them,
  And can still employ them,
  Our mind and senses and our every member,
  Thanks do we owe for this let us remember.
Praise ye Jehovah!
[280]
By flames o'erpowering,
  Us and ours devouring,
  From house and homestead that we've not been driven
  We owe it to the care of God in Heaven.
Praise ye Jehovah!
That no thief, breaking
  Through our doors and taking
  Our property, and us assaulting hurt us,
  Is that He sent His angels to support us.
Praise ye Jehovah!
Oh, faithful Saviour!
  Fount of every favour!
  Ah! let Thy kindness and protection hover,
  By day and night our life at all times over.
Praise ye Jehovah!
Deign, Lord, to hear us,
  And to-day be near us!
  Supported by Thy grace, may nought e'er hinder
  Our progress; and, in need, help speedy render.
Praise ye Jehovah!
[281]
Our will subduing,
  Make us Thine be doing,
  Teach us to labour faithfully; whenever
  Beneath the load we're sinking, then deliver.
Praise ye Jehovah!
Do Thou direct us
  When Thou dost afflict us,
  That we may never mock; but be

preparing
Before Thy throne hereafter for appearing.
Praise ye Jehovah!
And all true-hearted
Who're by grace converted
Wilt Thou, Lord, come for, and by grace be bringing
Where all Thine angels evermore are singing,
Praise ye Jehovah!
[282]

EVENING BLESSING.

The daylight disappeareth,
It fleeth, and night neareth,
Its gloom is spreading o'er us,
With slumber to o'erpower us
And all the wearied earth.
The working day now endeth,
My heart to Thee ascendeth,
For toil and rest who'st given
The morning and the even,—
In praise my heart bursts forth.
Break forth, my heart, in singing,
Praise to thy Maker bringing,
Who soul and body giveth,
More good than heart conceiveth,
Or tongue can ever tell;
No moment passeth over
That doth not much discover
Of goodness overflowing,
He's aye on us bestowing,
Each hour doth show it well.
[283]
Just as the shepherd's treasure,
The sheep in boundless pleasure
O'er greenest pastures wander,
Their guardian's guidance under,
With free and fearless mind,
Themselves with flowers filling,
Their thirst at fresh springs stilling,
So me to-day hath guided,
With every good provided,
My Shepherd, good and kind.
God hath not me forsaken,
Though I sin's course have taken,
Not fearing e'er to leave Him,
By waywardness to grieve Him,
And wound His Father-heart.
Let, Father, Thy zeal never
Burn 'gainst me, nor me sever
From Thee and from Thy blessing;
My doing and transgressing
Awake regret and smart.
[284]

Oh! hear me, Father, praying,
My waywardness and straying
From Thee, my evil doing,
Into the ocean throwing,
Forgive eternally.
But may Thine angels hover
Round me, and be my cover,
All evil from me keeping;
With Thee will I be sleeping,
I'll rise again with Thee.
Now may mine eyelids closing
Be peacefully reposing,
All free from care and sorrow,
Till on the golden morrow
I joyfully awake.
Thy wings shall shield me ever,
The enemy shall never
Thy flock and me endanger,
Whom day and night in anger
His prey he seeks to make.
[285]
When silent or when talking,
When sitting or when walking,
To Thee I'm wholly given,
Thou art my life from heaven,
This word is true and sore.
In every undertaking,
In sleeping hours and waking,
My fortress art Thou ever,
Thine arm doth aye deliver,
My bliss doth aye endure.

NOW SPREAD ARE EVENING'S SHADOWS.

Now spread are evening's shadows,
O'er forests, towns, and meadows,
And sleepeth ev'ry eye;
Awake my pow'rs and sing ye,
And pray'r and praises bring ye,
That your Creator please on high!
[286]
O Sun! where art thou vanish'd?
The night thy light hath banish'd,
The night of day the foe;
Go then, for now appeareth
Another Sun and cheereth
My heart—'tis Jesus Christ, my joy!
We've seen the day's declining,
The golden stars are shining
In yonder dark-blue sky.
There shall I be for ever
When God doth me deliver,
From this low vale of misery.
To rest the body hasteth,
Itself of clothes divesteth,
Type of mortality!

I'll put it off, and o'er me
Christ will the robe of glory
Throw, and of immortality!
[287]
Head, hands, and feet so tirèd
Are glad the day's expirèd,
That work comes to an end;
My heart be fill'd with gladness
That God from all earth's sadness,
And from sin's toil relief will send.
Lie down, my members tired
Upon your couch desirèd,
Lie down my wearied head!
A day and hour is nearing
They'll be for you preparing
Beneath the sod, a quiet bed.
Mine eyes scarce ope are keeping,
A moment—I'll be sleeping,
Where's body then and soul?
In grace Thy care then make me,
May evil ne'er o'ertake me,
Thou Shepherd Lord of Israel!
[288]
O Jesus, be my cover!
And spread both Thy wings over
Thy child, and shield Thou me!
Though Satan would devour me,
Let angels ever o'er me
Sing, "This child shall uninjur'd be!"
And you, my well belovèd!
Shall by no ill be movèd,
No danger shall betide.
God peaceful slumbers send you,
With golden arms defend you,
Send guardian angels to your side!

Miscellaneous.
[289]

SUMMER SONG.

Go forth, my heart, and seek delight
In this summer time so bright,
The bounties God displayeth,
The garden's splendour go and see,
Behold how God for me and thee
Them gorgeously arrayeth.
The trees with leaves are cover'd o'er,
The earth with carpet spreads her floor
Of green, all fresh and tender,
The tulip and narcissus wear
Attire of finer texture fair
Than Solomon in splendour.
The lark aspiring soars on high,
Flies from her cleft the dove so shy,
[290]

And seeks the woodland shadow;
   The nightingale with song so rare
   Delights and fills the ev'ning air
   O'er mountain, vale, and meadow.
Leads forth her little brood the hen,
   The stork builds near the haunts of men,
   And feed their young the swallows;
   The stag so swift, the roe so light
   Of foot, come bounding from the height
   Into the grassy hollows.
The brooklets murmur in the sand,
   And fringe the edge on either hand
   With myrtle rich in shadow;
   The shepherds and the sheep rejoice,
   In joy and mirth you hear their voice
   Sound from the neighb'ring meadow.
The bee through all the live-long hours,
   Unwearied roams among the flow'rs,
[291]
   Its precious stores to gather;
   The strong juice of the vine each hour
   Is ever gaining strength and pow'r
   This glorious summer weather.
While springeth fast the precious grain,
   The young and old exult again,
   Praise Him with all their powers,
   Whose benefits unceasing are,
   With gifts so manifold and rare
   Who human nature dowers.
I cannot rest, I never dare,
   In my Creator's gracious care
   My inmost soul rejoices,
   To God most High, when all things raise
   A song of universal praise,
   My voice shall join their voices.
Methinks it is so pleasant here,
   All things so beautiful appear
[292]
In this our poor world even;
   What will it be when earth we leave,
   And at its golden gates receive
   Glad welcome into Heaven?
What purest light, what ecstasy,
   Will in the Saviour's garden be!
   How will it sound when 'fore Thee,
   All with united heart and voice,
   Ten thousand seraphins rejoice
   And rev'rently adore Thee.
Ah! blessèd God, oh! were I there
   Before Thy throne, and did I bear
   My branch of palm victorious,
   As angels do, my voice I'd raise

Thine ever blessèd name to praise,
   In songs of triumph glorious.
But though I still am dwelling here,
   And still the body's burden bear,
[293]
Can I be silent?—Never!
   My heart, no matter where I be,
   Or here or there, shall bend to Thee,
   In adoration ever.
Help! Lord, my soul with blessings crown,
   With blessings that from Heav'n flow down,
   That I may blossom ever!
   And may the summer of Thy grace
   Cause fruits of faith to grow apace,
   Fruits that shall wither never.
And may Thy Spirit dwell in me,
   May I a good branch ever be
   Ingrafted in the Saviour!
   In Thine own garden may I be
   To Thy name's praise a goodly tree,
   Implanted by Thy favour!
Grant me Thy paradise to share,
   And more fruit may I ever bear
[294]
While I am going thither.
   Thine honour, Lord, to me is dear,
   Thee and Thee only shall I here
   And yonder serve for ever.

OCCASIONED BY GREAT AND UNSEASONABLE RAIN.

O God! who dost Heav'n's sceptre wield
   What is it that now makes our field,
   And everything that it doth bear,
   Such sad and ruin'd aspect wear?
Nought else, in truth, but that the band
   Of men from Thee on every hand
   Have fallen utterly away,
   Their guilt increasing every day.
They who as God's own property
   His name should praise continually,
   And of God's word should love the light,
   Like heathen are involv'd in night.
[295]
The Heav'ns are all with darkness clad,
   The firmament's clear light doth fade;
   We wait to see the light again
   At dawn of day, but wait in vain.
In ceaseless strifes involv'd men are,
   In every place is fearful war,
   In every corner hate and spite,

   Contentions every class delight.
The elements o'er all the land
   Are stretching out 'gainst us the hand,
   And troubles from the sea arise,
   And troubles come down from the skies.
It is a time of anguish sore,
   For hunted, plagued their time before
   The people are into the grave,
   No rest to them do they vouchsafe.
The source of joy becometh sad,
   The sun hath ceas'd to make us glad,
   And all at once the clouds descend,
   Shed tears that never seem to end.
[296]
Ah, child of man! go weep alone,
   Thy many grievous sins bemoan,
   Henceforward from thy crimes refrain,
   Repent, and be thou clean again.
Fall on thy knees, thyself now throw
   On God, that He may mercy show,
   That His deservèd wrath may be
   By Him to grace turn'd speedily.
He's faithful, and aye true will be,
   Nought else desireth but that we
   With reverence and godly fear
   To seek His mercy should draw near.
Ah! Father, Father, hear our cry,
   Redeem us, 'neath sin's yoke we lie,
   From out the world drawn may we be,
   And Thou Thyself turn us to Thee.
Subdue Thou our rebellious mood,
   And make us, sinners, pure and good;
   Whom Thou dost turn, soon turn'd is he,
   Who heareth Thee, is heard by Thee!
[297]
And let Thine eye now friendly be,
   The anguish'd cry that reacheth Thee
   From earth, from our sad hearts, O Lord,
   With gracious ear do Thou regard.
Wrath's black robe tear off with Thy hand
   And comfort Thou us and our land,
   And may the genial sun shine forth
   And ripen the fair fruits of earth.
And, Lord, as long as we may live
   Our daily bread in bounty give,
   And when the end of time we see
   The bread give of eternity!
[298]

THANKSGIVING FOR GRACIOUS SUNSHINE.

Now gone is all the rain,
  Rejoice my heart again,
  Sing after times of sadness
  To God thy Lord with gladness!
  Our God His heart hath turnèd
  Our pray'r He hath not spurnèd.
On sea and on our land
  Outstretchèd was His hand,
  In anger us addressing;
  He said, "Ye're aye transgressing,
  In ways of sin ye wander,
  Nor ever turn, nor ponder.
"So shall my Heaven's light
  Its countenance so bright
  With robe of blackness cover,
  With dark clouds be spread over;
  No longer shine in glory
  But shall be weeping o'er thee."
[299]
Appeas'd His wrath our sighs
  That to His ears did rise,
  For He forgetteth never
  His mercy that dures ever,
  His Spirit tow'rd us yearning,
  His anger ceas'd from burning.
The clouds away then sped,
  The path the damp winds tread,
  From whence the rain descended,
  Was clos'd, the torrents ended,
  And from the deeps of Heaven
  No waters more were given.
Now wearied field away
  Thy robe of sadness lay,
  Arise from out thy sadness
  And let us hear with gladness
  Thee songs of summer raising,
  Thy great Creator praising.
[300]
The glorious sun, see there,
  Comes forth again so fair,
  With blessings earth doth cover;
  Now all the rains are over,
  Hills, valleys are receiving
  Its wondrous beams life-giving.
The earth's reviv'd again;
  What drown'd was by the rain
  Will once again be living
  And precious fruit be giving,
  The fields good wheat forth bringing,
  In meadows grass be springing.
The trees so very fair
  Fruit-laden will stand there;
  From hill-sides like a river
  Will wine and oil flow ever;
  In warm and quiet weather
  Will bees their honey gather.
[301]
Our portion He will give
  Who in the Heav'ns doth live.
  He'll bounteously bestow it,
  We shall partake and know it;
  And what earth will supply us
  Will amply satisfy us.
God faithful is and true,
  His mercy's ever new,
  His anger soon is turnèd.
  He gives what we've ne'er earnèd
  He doth Himself discover
  To us, our sins looks over.
O man! direct thy ways,
  And all thou dost, to praise
  Thy Master's love and favour,
  So that thy heart may never
  His faithful heart be grieving,
  To Him offence be giving!
[302]

THE WONDERFUL ESTATE OF MATRIMONY.

Full of wonder, full of art,
  Full of wisdom, full of pow'r,
  Full of kindness, grace, and heart,
  Full of comfort flowing o'er,
  Full of wonder, still I say,
  Is Love's chaste and gentle sway.
Those who've never met before,
  Ne'er each other known nor seen,
  Never in the idlest hour
  Thus employ'd their thoughts have been,
  Yet whose hearts and hands in love
  Tieth God who lives above!
His child doth *this* father guide,
  That one traineth his each day,
  Each their special wind and tide
  Speed upon their sep'rate way,
[303]
When the time appointed's there,
  Lo! they're a well-mated pair!
Here grows up a prudent son,
  And a noble daughter there;
  One will be the other's crown,
  One the other's rest from care
  Each will be the other's light,
  But from both 'tis hidden quite,
Till it's pleasing in His sight
  Who the world holds in His pow'r,
  To all giveth what is right
  Freely in th' appointed hour;
  Then appears in word and deed
  What hath been by Him decreed.
Then Ahasuerus' eye
  First doth quiet Esther see;
  To where Sara peacefully
  Dwells, Tobias leadeth He;
  David then, with pliant will,
  Fetcheth prudent Abigail.
[304]
Jacob flees from Esau's face,
  And he meeteth Rachel fair;
  Joseph in a foreign place
  Serves, and winneth Asnath there;
  Moses did with Jethro stay,
  And bore Zipporah away.
Each one taketh, each doth find
  What the Lord doth choose for him;
  What in Heaven is design'd,
  Comes to pass on earth in time.
  And whatever happens thus
  Order'd wisely is for us.
This or that might better be,
  Oft this foolish thought is ours;
  But as midnight utterly
  Fails to be like noonday's hours,
  So the feeble mind of man
  God's great wisdom cannot scan.
Whom God joins together live,
  What the best is knoweth He,
[305]
Our thoughts only can deceive,
  His from all defects are free;
  God's work standeth firm for aye,
  When all other must decay.
Look at pious children who
  Enter'd have the holy state,
  How well for them God doth do,
  See what joys upon them wait;
  To their doings God doth send
  Evermore a happy end.
Of their virtues the renown
  Blossometh for evermore,
  As a shadow when is gone
  Of all other love the flow'r;
  When truth faileth everywhere,
  Their's still bloometh fresh and fair,
Fresh their love is evermore,
  Ever doth its youth renew,
  Love their table covers o'er,
  Sweetens all they say and do.
[306]
Love their hearts aye giveth rest,
  When they're burden'd and oppress'd.
Though things oft go crookedly,

Even then this love is still,
   Can the cross bear patiently,
   Thinking 'tis the Father's will.
   From this thought doth comfort taste,
   Better days will come at last
Meanwhile streams of blessing gives
   God with bounty rich and free,
   Mind and body He relieves,
   And the house too foundeth He;
   What is small and men despise,
   Makes He great and multiplies.
And when all is over here
   That the Lord designs in love,
   For His faithful children dear,
   Taketh them to courts above,
   And with great delight in grace
   Folds them in His warm embrace.
[307]
Now 'tis ever full of heart,
   Full of comfort flowing o'er,
   Full of wonder, full of art,
   Full of wisdom, full of pow'r,
   Full of wonder, still I say,
   Is love's chaste and gentle sway.
This song used to be sung in Germany after wedding dinners, and in some places on the way to church before solemnization.

SONG OF CONSOLATION FOR MARRIED CHRISTIANS.

Oh, Jesus Christ! how bright and fair
   The state of holy marriage where
   Thy blessing rich is given
   What gracious gifts Thou dost bestow,
   What streams of blessing ever flow
   Down from Thy holy heaven,
   When they
   True stay
   To Thee ever,
   Leave Thee never,
   Whose troth plighted,
   In one life have been united.
[308]
When man and wife are mated well,
   In harmony together dwell,
   Are faithful to each other,
   The streams of bliss flow constantly
   What bliss of angels is on high
   From hence may we discover;
   No storm,
   No worm
   Can destroy it,
   Can e'er gnaw it,
   What God giveth
To the pair that in Him liveth.
He giveth of His grace the boon,
   And in its bosom late and soon
   His own belov'd He keepeth,
   His arms He daily spreadeth o'er,
   Guards as a Father by His pow'r
   Us and our house, nor sleepeth.
   Still we
   Must be
   Here and thither
   Roaming ever,
[309]
Till He gives us
   Pious homes, and thus relieves us.
The husband's like a goodly tree
   Whose branches spread so fair and free;
   The wife a vine that giveth
   Much fruit, and nurtures what it bears,
   Whose fruit increaseth with the years,
   Fruit that remains and liveth.
   Jewel,
   All hail!
   Husband's treasure!
   House's pleasure!
   Crown of honour!
   On His throne God thinketh on her.
O wife! the Lord hath chosen thee
   That from thy womb brought forth should be
   The folk His church that buildeth;
   His wondrous work goes on for aye,
   The mighty word His mouth doth say,
   What thou beholdest, yieldeth,
[310]
   Sons fair
   Stand there,
   Daughters sitting
   Working, knitting,
   Finely spinning,
   And with art time wisely winning.
Be of good cheer, it was not we
   Who first this order did decree,
   It was a higher Father,
   Who lov'd and loveth us for aye,
   And from whose lips when griev'd each day
   We friendly counsel gather;
   Good end
   He'll send,
   What we're doing
   And pursuing,
   Or conceiving
   Wise and happy issue giving.
A time will come, it cannot fail,
   When we 'neath trials sore shall quail,
[311]
   And tears be freely flowing;
   To him who bears it patiently,
   By God's grace shall his sorrow be
   Turn'd into joy o'erflowing.
   Toil now,
   Wait thou,
   He arriveth
   Who rest giveth,
   Who can ever
   Banish care and soon deliver.
Come hither then, my King so bless'd!
   In trials guide, in pain give rest,
   In anxious times relieving!
   To Thee we shall ascribe the praise,
   Our hearts and voices we shall raise
   In one loud song, thanks giving,
   Till we
   With Thee
   Ever dwelling,
   And fulfilling
   Thy will ever,
   Thy name cease to praise shall never.

Of Death, the Last Day, and Eternal Life.
[312]

OF DEATH AND DYING.—PSALM XC.

Lord God! Thou art for evermore
   Thy people's habitation,
   And Thou existence hadst before
   Was laid the earth's foundation!
   Ere yet the hills began to be
   Thou lived'st in eternity,
   Of all things the beginning!
Thou lettest all the crowds of men
   Through death's dark portals wander,
   And biddest them return again,
   Those others follow yonder.
   With Thee a thousand years are aye
   Like watch of night or yesterday
   When it is gone for ever.
[313]
Thou lettest the base hosts of men
   E'en as a stream be flowing,
   And as a ship upon the main
   That fav'ring winds are blowing,
   And as a sleep and dream of night
   That when men wake at morning light

They can no more remember.
We're like an herb that early dies,
   Or grass in fields that groweth,
   That in the morning flourishes,
   Ere night the mower moweth.
   So is't with man: he blooms to-day,
   To-morrow he is borne away
   If but a breath doth touch him!
Because Thy wrath 'gainst us doth glow,
   Lord! we so early vanish,
   And for our sins Thou lay'st us low,
   And from Thy face dost banish.
   Our sins Thou sett'st before Thine eyes,
   Then doth Thine indignation rise
   In Thine heart ever holy!
[314]
This fire it is consumes in all
   Our bones the marrow ever;
   And hence it is that great or small
   From death escapeth never.
   And hence our days are passing o'er
   Like tales that oft beguile an hour
   And that are soon forgotten.
And scarcely doth our life on earth
   To seventy years last even;
   And what are all our labours worth
   If four-score years be given.
   What is the sum of all our gain
   From youth to age, but toil and pain,
   Heart-sorrow and vexation?
We're ever toiling full of care,
   And ere we do bethink us
   To stop our work, lo! death is there,
   Into the grave to sink us.
   And speedily we pass away,
   Yet of their end none ever stay
   To think, nor of God's anger.
[315]
O teach us, Lord! to think each day
   Upon this earth's affliction,
   That when we think on death we may
   Grow wiser by reflection.
   Ah! turn on us again Thy face
   And be at peace, O God of grace!
   With Thy rebellious children.
And early with Thy mercy free
   Be soul and body filling,
   And late and early, Lord, may we
   Thy glorious praise be telling.
   O chiefest joy! our hearts now cheer,
   And once more give us good times here,
   The days have been so evil.

We've borne the cross these weary years,
   Now let Thy sun be shining,
   Vouchsafe us laughter after tears,
   And pleasure after pining.
   And evermore, O Lord! make known
   Thy works of wonder to Thine own,
   Thine honour to Thy children.
[316]
Be Thou our faithful friend and God,
   Establish us for ever!
   And when we err from wisdom's road
   Give penitence and favour!
   Turn Thou our hearts again to Thee,
   May all our works establish'd be,
   Crown all we do with blessing!

A REST HERE HAVE I NEVER.—PS. CXIX.

A rest here have I never,
   A guest on earth am I,
   Heav'n will be mine for ever,
   My Fatherland's on high.
   Here up and down I'm driven;
   In rest eternal there,
   God's gift of grace is given
   That endeth toil and care.
What hath my whole life ever
   From youth been to this hour,
   But labour ceasing never,
   As long as I have pow'r
[317]
To tell of; days of anguish
   I've past, and oft the night
   In sorrow did I languish
   Until the morning light.
And on the ways I've wander'd
   What storms have terrified,
   It blew, rain'd, lighten'd, thunder'd,
   Fear was on every side.
   Hate, envy, opposition
   Rag'd, undeserv'd by me,
   This was the sad condition
   I must bear patiently.
So liv'd the honour'd fathers
   In whose footsteps we tread,
   From whom the saint oft gathers
   The wisdom he may need
   Of trial what full measure
   Had father Abraham,
   Ere he attain'd his pleasure,
   To his right dwelling came.
[318]
How rough too and uneven
   The way that Isaac trod,

And Jacob, who had striven
   And had prevail'd with God;
   What bitter grief and wearing
   Felt he, what woe and smart;
   In fear and in despairing
   Oft sank his fainting heart.
The holy souls and blessèd
   Went forward on their race,
   They chang'd with hearts distressèd
   Their wonted dwelling-place:
   They hither went and thither,
   Great crosses bore each day,
   Till death came to deliver,
   Them in the grave to lay.
In patience am I giving
   Myself to just such woe?
   Could I be better living
   Than such have liv'd below?
[319]
Here must we suffer ever,
   Here must we upwards strive;
   Who fights not well shall never
   In joy eternal live.
While on the earth I'm staying,
   My life shall thus be spent,
   I would not be delaying
   For aye in this strange tent.
   Along the paths I wander
   That lead me to my home,
   God boundless comfort yonder
   Will give me when I come.
My home is high above me,
   Where angel hosts for aye
   Praise Him whose heart doth love me,
   Who ruleth all each day,
   Who aye preserves and beareth
   All in His hand of might,
   Who orders and prepareth
   What good seems in His sight.
[320]
For home my tir'd heart yearneth,
   I'd gladly thither go,
   From earth away it turneth
   From all I've here pass'd through.
   The longer here I'm staying
   I less of pleasure taste,
   My spirit's thirst allaying,
   The world's an arid waste.
The dwelling is unholy,
   The trouble is too great.
   Why com'st Thou, Lord, so slowly
   To free me from this state?
   Come, make a happy ending
   Of all my wanderings,

Relief by Thy pow'r sending,
    From all my sufferings.
Where I've so long remainèd
  Is not my proper home;
  When my life's end is gainèd,
  Then forth from it I'll come,
[321]
What here I've needed ever
  I'll put it all away;
  When soul and body sever,
  Me in the grave they'll lay.
Thou, who my Joy art ever,
  And of my life the Light,
  When death life's thread doth sever,
  Bring'st me to heav'n so bright,
    To mansions everlasting,
    Where I shall ever shine,
  E'en as the sun, while tasting
    Of pleasures all divine.
There I'll be ever living
  Not merely as a guest,
  With those who crowns receiving
  From Thee are ever bless'd;
  I'll celebrate in glory
  Thine ev'ry mighty deed,
  My portion have before Thee,
  From every evil freed.
[322]

CHRISTIAN JOY IN DEATH.

My face, why should'st thou troubled be
  When thou of death art hearing?
  Know it, it cannot injure thee,
  Contemplate it, ne'er fearing.
  When thou dost know
  Death, all its woe
  Will soon be disappearing.
From the old serpent's face first tear
  The mask he is assuming,
  And lo! no poison more is there,
  'Tis harmless through the coming
  Of Christ to save,
  Who to the grave
  Went down, death thus o'ercoming.
[323]
Thou, Lord, didst break our foe's great pow'r,
  His sting thus from him taking,
  The butt of scorn he's evermore,
  No mischief can be making.
  Thy precious blood
  Damps his hot mood,
  His ardour's him forsaking.
'Twas sin that was the sting of death,
  And on to dying drove us,
  For ever done away sin hath
  Our Saviour, who did love us.
  Its pow'r and might
  Is broken quite,
  Though it to grief may move us.
Now sin is dead, God's anger's turn'd,
  He's reconcil'd; the Saviour
  Hath borne the curse our debts had earn'd,
  Restor'd us to God's favour.
  Who was our foe
  Our friend is now,
  Is full of grace for ever.
[324]
It cannot be, if Thou'rt my friend,
  That Thou would'st kill me ever;
  Thy Father's heart can ne'er intend
  To death me to deliver,
  And who is e'er
  Thy child and heir
  By ill is injur'd never.
But Thou, O Father! doest well
  When trials sore are grieving,
  When misery the life doth fill,
  The waves around us heaving,
  That us Thy hand
  To Fatherland
  Brings, from the floods relieving.
When from the angry skies storms break,
  And mountains quake before them,
  The thunder of Thy wrath doth shake
  The hills, and pealeth o'er them,
  Then dost Thou come
  And takest home
  Thine own, Thou carest for them.
[325]
When rage around our enemies,
  Our injury are seeking,
  When lions, wolves, and bears arise,
  Their vengeance on us wreaking,
  Thou tak'st Thy sheep,
  Dost safely keep
  Them near Thee, comfort speaking.
And if the world treats evilly
  Him who to Thee is cleaving,
  Thou sayest, "Come to me, my son!
  Come, from me be receiving
  Love, pleasure, joy,
  That never cloy,
  That I for aye am giving."
And angel hosts then joyfully
  Descend, and round us hover,
  And tend the soul so carefully;
  And when life's course is over
    To God on high
    It peacefully
  Goes with them 'neath their cover.
[326]
The Lord His bride meets joyfully
  And saith, "Now welcome ever,
  I have espousèd thee to me,
  To all mine own come hither!
  Whom I 'fore thee
  Have brought to me,
  From yon world did deliver.
"Thou true and faithful wast in heart,
  Wast ne'er asham'd to own me,
  And now receivest thou thy part,
  With crown of joy I crown thee.
  Thy part am I,
  Eternally
  Beside me I enthrone thee.
"Of thine eyes now I dry the flood,
  Thy bitter tears am stilling;
  Here turn'd is to thy highest good,
  The grief thou once wert feeling;
  Of thy grief's sea
  No one shall be
  Here save with rapture telling.
[327]
"All my belov'd ones clothe I here
  In pure white linen ever,
  With joy in heaven they appear,
  Here envy felt is never.
  Here is no death,
  No cross nor scath,
  Good friends at all can sever."
O God! why should the thought of death
  With terror make me shiver?
  'Tis he who'll from the yoke beneath
  Of mis'ry me deliver.
  From torture He
  Will set me free,
  I can regret it never.
For death is the Red Sea to me,
  Through which on dry land ever
  Thine Israel, so dear to Thee,
  Pass to the land of favour,
  Where milk and wine
  Flow ever in
  Full streams that cease shall never.
[328]
It is heav'n's golden door to me,
  The fiery car God sendeth,
  Wherein my spirit speedily
  To th' angel choir ascendeth,
  When God shall say
  "Thy working day
  Of life below now endeth."

O sweetest joy, O blessèd rest!
 To all true-hearted given,
 Come, let mine eyes by Thee be press'd,
 In peace take me to heaven.
 May I roam there
 'Mong pastures fair
 Where day ne'er knoweth even.
What fails us here, there will He give,
 Full measure to us bringing,
 Our grateful songs shall He receive,
 From loving hearts up-springing.
 And there shall I
 Too, willingly
 Song after song be singing.
[329]

JOYFUL RESIGNATION TO A HAPPY DEPARTURE FROM THIS WEARY WORLD.

Be glad, my heart! now fear no more,
 Let nothing ever grieve thee;
 Christ lives, who lov'd thee long before
 Thy being He did give thee,
 And ere He made thy wondrous frame;
 His love remaineth still the same,
 It ne'er can change to hatred.
Be of good cheer! thy nearing end,
 My heart! need not appal thee,
 No ill's in it; God doth extend,
 His loving hand and call thee
 From all the thousand forms of woe
 That in this vale of tears below,
 Thou ever hast endurèd.
[330]
'Tis true, 'tis call'd death's agony,
 But yet it is no dying;
 The death of death is Christ, for He
 Prevents it from destroying,
 That though it puts forth all its pow'r,
 No hair it hurteth in the hour
 When I from hence am taken.
The sting of death in sin doth lie,
 And in our evil doing;
 Poor child of Adam! eagerly
 This path was I pursuing.
 In Christ's blood sin is wash'd away,
 Forgiven are we now for aye,
 Ne'er fall in condemnation.
My sin is gone, and I am clean,
 Whoever would deprive me,
 Henceforth is life eternal mine;
 The thought may never grieve me
 Of sin's dread wages earn'd by me;
 Who's reconcil'd, must ever be,
 Unhurt by opposition.
[331]
Now God's free grace I with me take,
 And all His joy and gladness,
 On this last journey that I make,
 And know no grief nor sadness.
 The foe becomes to me a sheep,
 His ire becomes a blessèd sleep,
 Of quiet rest the pillow.
Thou Jesus! O thou sweetest Friend,
 My light and life art ever!
 Thou holdest me, dost me defend,
 The foe can move Thee never.
 In Thee I am, Thou art in me,
 As we are here, we'll ever be,
 Nought here or there can part us.
My body down to rest doth lie,
 Fatigued with life's sad story;
 The soul then mounteth up on high,
 With chosen ones in glory
 It mingles, and keeps joyfully,
 The endless year of Jubilee
 With all the holy angels.
[332]
Oh! Highest Prince of great and small,
 May that bless'd day be nearing;
 When Thou shalt by Thy trumpet call,
 And all the dead be hearing.
 Again shall soul and body be
 One, and Thy joy shall taste and see,
 Thy Father's kingdom enter.
If 'tis Thy will, O Lord, appear,
 To peace and bliss to take me
 For ever, Thee may I be near,
 How joyful would it make me!
 Be open'd wide—of death, thou gate!
 That to so bliss'd place and state
 Through thee I may pass over.
[333]

THE BEREAVED FATHER COMFORTS HIMSELF CONCERNING HIS NOW SAINTED SON.

Mine art thou still, and mine shalt be,
 Who will be this denying?
 Not only thou belong'st to me,
 The Lord of Life undying
 The greatest right hath aye in thee;
 He taketh, He demands from me
 Thee, O my son, my treasure,
 My heart's delight and pleasure!
If wish avail'd, my soul's sweet star!
 My free choice would I make thee,
 Than earth's fair treasures rather far,
 I evermore would take thee.
 Would say to thee, Abide with me,
 The joy of all my dwelling be,
 I ever more shall love thee,
 Till death itself remove me.
[334]
Thus saith my heart, and meaneth well,
 But God doth mean still better;
 Great love doth in my bosom dwell,
 In God there dwelleth greater.
 I am a father, nothing more,
 Of fathers God's the crown and pow'r,
 The fountain who is giving
 Their being to all living.
I long and yearn for my dear son;
 God, by whom he was given,
 Wills he should stand beside His throne,
 Should live with Him in heaven.
 I say, Alas! my light is gone!
 God saith, "I welcome thee, my son,
 I'd have thee ever near me,
 With endless joys would cheer thee!"
O lovely word! O sweet decree!
 More holy than we ever
 Can think; with God no ill can be,
 Mischance, or sickness never,
[335]
No care, no want, no oversight,
 With God no sorrow e'er can blight;
 Whom God cares for and loveth
 No trouble ever moveth.
We men much thought and time expend
 On our dear ones' adorning;
 Our thoughts and efforts ever bend,
 Are planning night and morning
 To gain for them a happy place;
 And yet how seldom 'tis the case
 They reach the destination
 We had in contemplation.
How oft a young and hopeful one
 From virtue's path far roameth,
 By him through ill example's done
 What Christians ne'er becometh.
 Then God's just anger doth he earn,
 On earth he meeteth scoffs and scorn,
 His father's heart he filleth
 With pain that nothing stilleth.
[336]
Now such can never be my case,
 My son is safely yonder,
 Appeareth now before God's face,
 Doth in Christ's garden wander,

Is fill'd with joy, is ever bless'd,
And from heart-sorrow doth he rest,
Sees, hears the hosts so glorious
Who here are watching o'er us.
He angels yonder hears and sees,
  Part in their songs he taketh,
And knows all wisdom's mysteries;
  His high discourse he maketh
What none of us can ever know
With all our searching here below,
  To none on earth 'tis given,
  Reserv'd it is for Heaven.
Ah! could I even draw so near,
  Could it to me be given
The faintest sounds of praise to hear
  That fill the courts of Heaven,
[337]
When prais'd is the thrice holy One,
  Who thee hath sanctified, my son!
Joy would my heart be swelling,
  Tears from mine eyes be welling.
Would I then say, Stay with me here,
  Henceforth I'll murmur never;
Alas! my son! wert thou but near!
  No, but come quickly hither
Thou fiery car, and take me where
My child and all the blessèd are,
  Who speak of things so glorious,
  O'er every ill victorious.
Now be it so, I'd have it so,
  I'll never more deplore thee;
Thou liv'st, pure joys thy heart o'erflow,
  Bright suns shine ever o'er thee,
  The suns of endless joy and rest.
Live then, and be for ever bless'd,
  I shall, when God wills, yonder
  In bliss hereafter wander.
[338]

BY THE BIER OF A FRIEND.

On thy bier how calm thou'rt sleeping
  Yet thou livest, oh our crown!
Watch eternal art thou keeping,
  Standing near thy Saviour's throne.
Endless joy thy portion now!
Why should tears so freely flow?
  What should thus in sorrow sink us?
  Up! aright let us bethink us!
Grudge we to our friends their pleasure;
  When they laugh, we laugh again;
Bitter tears shed without measure,
  When we see them sunk in pain.
When we see them conq'rors come,
From the cross triumphant home;
  When is o'er life's toil and anguish,
  Then no more in grief we languish.
[339]
Noble heart! in peace now rest thee,
  Thou hast vanquish'd every foe,
All afflictions that oppress'd thee,
  Overwhelm'd thy heart with woe;
All the toil and misery,
All care and anxiety,
  All that made thee sleep in sorrow,
  Wake in anguish on the morrow.
God who sendeth all temptations,
  Knows the burden each can bear;
He appoints all tribulations,
  Who in loving, gracious care,
Sent thee every trial sore
That thou now hast triumphed o'er,
  Who hath strength enough to bear it,
  Must in larger measure share it.
Hadst thou been at heart a craven,
  Shrinking from the chilly blast,
Loving most the quiet haven,
  With no cloud the sky o'ercast,
[340]
God, the giver of all good,
  Never such a grievous load
Of affliction had ordain'd thee,
  As dishearten'd oft and pain'd thee.
Triumph now, for thou, victorious
  By the pow'r of God most high,
Sonlike in thy strength so glorious,
  Walk'st amid the Company
Of the city fair and new,
Which the Lord hath built for you;
  With the angels join'st in singing,
  Sweetest songs from heart up-springing.
Jesus bids thee cease from weeping
  Wipes the tear-drop from thine eye;
Free thy heart from sorrow keeping
  All thy need doth He supply.
In thy cup now running o'er
Wishest thou but one thing more,
  That thy friends who here still wander
  Were thy bliss now sharing yonder.
[341]
To the realms we'll come so glorious,
  Out of sorrow into joy;
Thee with myriad saints victorious
  See in bliss without alloy.
Oh! how bless'd and fair 'twill be,
When we all shall dwell with Thee;
  When is o'er life's chequer'd story,
  And we reign in endless glory.

OF THE LAST DAY.

The time is very near
  When, Lord, Thou wilt be here
The signs whereof Thou'st spoken
Thine advent should betoken,
  We've seen them oft fulfilling
  In number beyond telling.
What shall I do then, Lord?
  But rest upon Thy word,
The promise Thou hast given
That Thou wilt come from heaven,
  Me from the grave deliver
  And from all woe for ever.
[342]
Ah! Jesus Christ, how fair
  Wilt be my portion there!
The welcome Thou'lt address me,
Thy glances, how they'll bless me,
  When I the earth forsaking,
  My flight to Thee am taking.
Ah! what will be the word
  Thou'lt speak, my Shepherd Lord!
What will be then Thy greeting,
Me and my brethren meeting?
  Thy members Thou wilt own us,
  And near Thyself enthrone us.
And in that blessèd hour,
  How shall I have the pow'r
Mine eyelids dry of keeping,
How tears of joy from weeping
  Refrain, that flowing over
  My cheeks, like floods would cover?
[343]
And what a beauteous light
  Will from Thy face so bright
Beam on me, then in heaven,
When sight of Thee is given,
  Thy goodness then me filling,
  Joy will my breast be swelling.
I'll see then and adore
  Thy body bruisèd sore,
Whereon our faith is founded,
The prints of nails that wounded
  Thy hands and feet be greeting,
  Thy gaze with rapture meeting.
Thou, Lord, alone dost know
  The joys so pure that flow
In life's unfailing river
In paradise for ever,
  Thou can'st portray, and show them:
  By faith alone I know them.
[344]
What I've believ'd stands sure,
  Remaineth aye secure;
My part the wealth surpasseth;

The richest here amasseth;
All other wealth decayeth
My portion ever stayeth.
My God, my fairest Part!
How will my bounding heart
With joy be overflowing,
Praise evermore renewing,
When through the door of heaven
By Thee is entrance given?
Thou'lt say, "Come, taste and see,
Oh! child, belov'd by me,
Come, taste the gifts so precious
I and my Father gracious
Have to bestow, come hither,
In pleasure bask for ever."
[345]
Alas! thou world so poor!
Of wealth, what is thy store?
Mean is it to be holden,
Compar'd with all the golden
Crowns and thrones Jesus placeth
For whom He loves and graceth.
Here is the angel's home,
Bless'd spirits hither come,
Here nought is heard but singing,
Nought seen but joy up-springing,
No cross, no death, no sorrow,
No parting on the morrow.
Hold! hold! my sense so weak!
What dost thou think and speak,
What's fathomless, art sounding?
What's measureless, art bounding?
Here must man's wit be bending
The eloquent be ending.
[346]
Lord! I delight in Thee,
Thou ne'er shalt go from me,
Thy hand in bounty giveth
More than my heart conceiveth,
Or I can e'er be counting,
So high Thy mercy's mounting.
How sad, O Lord, am I,
Until I from on high
See Thee in glory hither
Come, Thine own to deliver,
Wert Thou but now revealing
Thyself! my wish fulfilling!
The time is known to Thee;
It best becometh me
To be prepar'd for going,
And all things so be doing,
That every moment even
My heart may be in Heaven.
[347]
This grant, Lord, and me bless.

That so Thy truth and grace
May keep me ever waking,
That Thy day not o'ertaking
Me unawares, affright me,
But may, O Lord! delight me.

FROM THE REVELATION OF JOHN.—CHAP. VII.

By John was seen a wondrous sight,
A noble light,
A picture very glorious:
A multitude stood 'fore him there
All bright and fair,
On heav'nly plain victorious;
Their heart and mood
Were full of good,
That mortal man
With gold ne'er can
Procure, so high 'tis o'er us.
[348]
Palm branches in their hands they bore,
They stood before
The Lamb's throne, 'fore the Saviour;
Praise from their lips did ever flow,
Their robes like snow,
Their song still higher ever,
So sweetly rang;
Glad thanks they sang,
And in their song
The holy throng
Of angels joinèd ever.
"Who," said the wond'ring John, "are they
In white array,
Whom now I see before me?"
"They are," said one from out the crowd
That round him stood,
One of the elders hoary,
"They're men, my son,
Who fought and won
The fight of faith,
Despis'd the scath,
Attain'd the prize of glory.
[349]
"They're those who on the earth below,
Long, long ago,
Pass'd through great tribulation;
Who for the honour of their Lord
And of His word,
All grief and all vexation,
From blame all free
But patiently,
Though smarting sore
By God's help bore,

O'ercame with exultation.
"They wash'd their robes and made them white
(Their hearts were right),
In faith's bath them renewing,
And they resisted evermore
With all their pow'r
Hell's art, it quite subduing,
Did aye deride
Earth's pomp and pride,
Chose Jesu's blood
As their chief good,
All other good eschewing.
[350]
"And therefore with their doings, they
Stand there for aye,
Where God's fair temple's standing,
The temple where they night and day
Praise God for aye,
His glorious name commending.
There do they live
With nought to grieve,
From toil all free
Joys taste and see,
That never know an ending.
"There in His dwelling sitteth God
And spreads abroad
His goodness as a cover,
There with bliss manifold is bless'd
In quiet rest,
The wearied whose life's over;
What pleasure gives,
The heart relieves,
The longing stills,
And the eye fills,
In full bloom stands there ever.
[351]
"No thirst, nor hunger there, no need;
The heav'nly bread
All wants aye satisfieth;
And shineth there the sun no more
In too great pow'r,
Its light pure joy supplieth;
Heav'n's sun so bright
And heart's delight,
Is our great Lord
The living Word,
Who no good thing denieth."
The Lamb His flock will ever feed
E'en as they need,
In pastures never wasting;
He will them to the fountain bring,
Whence ever spring
Streams of life everlasting;
And certainly

Ne'er rest will He,
Till wash'd away
All tears for aye
Are, and His bliss we're tasting.

LONDON:
PRINTED BY W. CLOWES AND SONS, STAMFORD STREET AND CHARING CROSS.